BE GENEROUS AND PROSPER
REFLECTIONS ON HOW YOU CAN SAVE THE WORLD

Sebastian Nybo with H. H. Dalai Lama

Be generous and prosper

Reflections on how you can save the world

Literary Guides
Pernille Kienle and Paul McNeice

Sebastian Nybo with His Holiness the Dalai Lama
Be generous and prosper – reflections on how you can save the world

© 2010 Sebastian Nybo and Origo Ltd.
Cover: Bohemian A/S
Photo: Henrik Cliffort
Type: Janus René Andersen
BOD
1st issue, 1st print, 2010
ISBN 978-87-990593-2-4

Origo Ltd.
Nygade 6, 4th floor
1164 Copenhagen
Denmark
Telephone: +45-3311-4422

sn@wisdominaction.nu
www.oneglobeonepeople.com
No part of this book may be reproduced
in any form or by any electronic or mechanical means
without written permission from Origo Ltd.

Table of contents

THANK YOU — 7

THE MASTER AND HIS STUDENT — 9

INTRODUCTION — 13
Ethical dilemmas are similar around the globe • Ocean of Buddhist wisdom • The corporate world – the key to radical change • The code of knighthood • It is all about Love • No need for at spiritual go-between • What is the recipe for a human being? • Ethics are in our genes

ANTS ARE MORE IMPORTANT THAN US — 24
Capitalism version 2.0 – in which we spend our lives longing for things we do not really need • The 'Doomsday Clock' is ticking • Change is good – total transformation is better • World Inc. is under severe pressure • Equation for change • Crossroads • We are one people • Overpopulation and natural migration • Are we programmed for cultural diversity?

HISTORY – SOMETHING THAT YOU CAN LEARN FROM — 36
The ostrich attitude • How did it come to this? • Absurd juxtapositions • The richest 400's wealth is equal to the 3,7 billion poorest • We see what we believe we see … not what is • Are we a self-destructive species? • On a larger scale

WE DO HAVE THE NECESSARY RESOURCES — 48
The windblown trees of the west coast • We are told different stories

THE RIGID MIND — 56
The Lottery of Life – what did you get? • Waking up to reality

ETHICS – OUR PSYCHOLOGICAL BACKBONE 64
Equality is an absolute core ethic • Business ethics

THE NEXT LEAP IN EVOLUTION: HOMO SPIRITUALIS 69
Our internal homing device • God, eternity and all that • New wine in old bottles? • Science 'grants' us eternal life • Eternity can cause laziness • The Lotus flower • The humble prophets • We already know

MAKING A DIFFERENCE 77
Radical innovation is needed

COURAGE TO CHANGE WHAT I CAN 82
Meditation – a way to freedom • Release your talent • Our internal ethical navigation system • Intellect, emotions and intuition – the perfect triad • How to release your intuition • What is the cure? • We are the sum of our actions

WISDOM IN ACTION 93
The four principles for a sustainable future • Give and be blessed • Non-violence • Do not kill • The Code for Ethical Humans

CHANGE THROUGH WORK AND BUSINESS 101
Pure business • Why change the world through business • 'You must be very scared' • It's about our survival • Complexity poses new demands • Change from the inside out • Guidelines for Ethical Business Owners • The myth of 'Only the strong survive'

TRUE LEADERSHIP 112
Inspiration • The old lion • Guidelines for those who lead others • Honest work • Guidelines for the Ethical Employee

CONCLUSION: THE TIME FOR CONVENIENT TREACHERY IS OVER 123
The world is a small place • Utopia • There is hope • It is a mystery to live • A New Dawn • Life is yours to live – for ever and ever

REFERENCES 139

AUTHOUR BIOGRAPHIES 142

Thank you

First of all I wish to thank His Holiness the 14th Dalai Lama for devoting so much of his time to discuss these complicated matters with me. I am grateful for the warmth, understanding and insight he showed me during those three otherwise very cold days in Dharamsala in northern India.

I also wish to extend a thanks to Lakha Lama for encouraging me to write this book – I don't think he realizes what a journey this project would turn out to be for me – or, perhaps he knew all along. Lakha Lama was the first lama I encountered, because he lives in my home country of Denmark. He quickly became a great source of inspiration to me when he opened the gates to the wisdom of the Tibetan culture and Buddhist philosophy to me. Later on, he was the one who arranged my dialogs and my meetings with His Holiness the Dalai Lama.

Having thanked the two Lamas, who have both played a crucial part in the creation of this book, I also wish to thank those, who have helped me write and produce the book. On that note, I wish to thank my English literary guide, Paul McNeice for taking the time for the many in-depth discussions about anything from spelling to proper syntax. Also thank you to Pernille Kienle for your corrections and final shaping of the English version. Thanks to my assistant, Marianne Petersen, who helped me write out the many hours of dialog with His Holiness the Dalai Lama and, who also assisted in the first revision, which was not an easy task. You showed such devotion and dedication to this assignment.

Christian Have – thank you for your sparring on the first draft and for your support and help when I suffered from writer's block – and for your friendship, which means so much to me.

I also wish to thank my dear friend and linguistic critic, Dinke van Damme, who spent ten days with me, non-stop, in a wind-blown summer house in North Zealand where, at times, it was stormier inside than outside. Thank you for enduring it.

A profound thank you to my sister, Pernille, and her husband, Stiig, for showing me what unconditional love is and for giving me an insight into the challenges you face from all directions, even from those who were supposed to help you. You never give up – because your children's needs are more important than anything – and I admire you for that.

In addition, I wish to thank my Danish publisher, Kastaniehøj, Anja Desirée Lykkeberg, who in addition to editing the Danish version of the book, prompted me to collect the ethic cases that are now included in the book. These help clarify that everyone, regardless of their position, rank or social conditions, can make an active effort for a better and more socially fair, sustainable future for the Earth.

The master and his student

It was late in the afternoon. The master was sitting alone in the atrium in deep meditation. The last rays of sunlight were caressing his face. Everything around him was bathed in a dozy golden glow. He was peaceful – breathing calmly and silently. It almost seemed as if the peace came from inside of him and spread to the surroundings; as if he were the center of the peace, rather than merely its beholder.

It was utterly quiet in the atrium. Time was standing still like a dragonfly that hovers above a lake on a warm summer afternoon. The door seemed to creak louder than it actually did when one of his young students entered. He approached the master as quietly as he could. It was obvious that the young student would have preferred not to disturb, yet something inside him was stirring. It was difficult for him to remain calm. In respect of the master's deep meditation he sat down at an appropriate distance and waited. He waited for his master to open his half-closed eyes and call for him. Before long, however, his impatience made him clear his throat – very quietly. No response from the master. So he coughed again – louder this time. Still, no response. He ended up coughing so loudly that it echoed slightly from the colonnade that wrapped around the atrium. Only then did the master finally open up his eyes and look at him.

With a gesture the master indicated for the student to come and sit with him, which he quickly did. Once the master saw that the student was comfortable he said, 'Something inside you is in a hurry.'

The young man looked at the master and said, 'The world is in pain. So much needs to be changed. No matter where I look, I see oppression, humiliation and poverty. I see the degradation of injustice in the eyes of the victims. I see the greed in the dough-like faces of the rich. Animals are being perceived as mere products and tortured. The Earth and the air are being polluted in the self-centered, complacent shadow of thoughtlessness. The unconscious warrior is still raging – spreading death, pain and suffering. Why have I been given this ability to see so clearly what is wrong and unjust, but not the ability to change it? Eventhough I do my utmost to help, my efforts are nothing but a drop in the ocean. Every night I fall down on my bed, exhausted. My inadequacy is torturing me. It never lets me find peace, because there is so much more that needs to be done.' Tears rolled down the student's cheeks as he continued, 'Every time I sit down to eat I envision the hungry, and every time I rest I envision the poor slaving for a lump of bread. So now I ask you, my wise master, what more can I do than I already am, because it is by far not enough? Time is precious because every second that I do nothing means that humanity is suffering.'

The master leaned forward. He took the young student's hands and said, 'When I was a young man I, too, wanted to change and save the entire world; and that is a beautiful wish. However, it is also a selfish wish, driven by ego. It is not for one person alone to save the entire human race – for only the individual can truly save himself.

When I was a little older it seemed right to help the people that were close to me. I learned that if by helping, you make the person you help passive; it is only a different kind of oppression.

Today I am old and I have realized that saving oneself is

most important of all. It is also the only one you truly can save. All deliverance in the world is essentially about liberating yourself. Therefore, my advice to you is to do the best you can with the resources you have – every day. No more, no less. But remember to also let happiness vitalize your soul. Otherwise it won't be long before you are unable to do anything for anyone. Observe how neither the sun nor the rain alone can bring life. They work together. The same way you must learn to weave together your joy and sorrow to rejuvenate the creative power and become part of the tireless Will. Life is magical and full of love. That is your nourishment, your source, and your point of origin. It is in light, love and joy that you will find the strength to enter the darkness, the injustice, and the cruelty.

Do the best you can. When you do that, without considering how much or how little it matters, you will be surrounded by bliss – like a protective blanket a mother wraps around her sleeping child. Then you are part of the stream of life as any truly co-creating human being. You will be nurtured by the warmth of your own inner sun and be able to gather the courage to fully unleash your unique potential. Then all life on Earth will benefit because of you.'

On the other side of right and wrong is a place;
I will meet you there.

(Rumi)

Introduction

*'Do not live in the past and do not dream about the future.
Focus your mind on the present.'*
(Buddha)

Today we need to apply these words of wisdom more than ever before. Mankind has created a world order that has devastating effects on the environment, animals and ourselves, to say the least. We must face up to the challenges that we and the Earth are facing – there is no excuse for not doing anything about it.

Because we are no longer innocents protected by our ignorance of the past. We know that it is not enough to dream of a glorious future. That it takes more than just good intentions to create a world where all beings live in harmony with each other and with the environment. And we know that there is a lot for us to do.

The clock is ticking. Look around you. Watch the news. Can you sense the urgency for global transformation?

All across the globe disasters are occurring which demonstrate the need for change: Tsunamis, hurricanes, global warming, overpopulation, pollution, civil wars, epidemics and the centralization of power with a handful of multinationals.

Democracy is spread too thin, extreme poverty is on the rise and the absurdly unfair distribution of the world's wealth and resources creates hopelessness and despair for billions of poor people. We need to face up to this and take action, and we need to do it now.

Ethical dilemmas are similar around the globe

My fascination with humankind and our sometimes very peculiar behavior has caused me to travel the world, and I have been extremely privileged to meet and learn from many wise and inspirational human beings. Even among these wise people, I found the Lamas of Tibet and their enduring adherence to the principles of non-violence to be exceptional.

The idea to write this book originated from a meeting in Copenhagen where the Dalai Lama and Rinpoche Lakha Lama – who is the leader of the Danish Tibetan Buddhism society – discussed how to raise global awareness about ethics and human decency. Rinpoche Lakha asked His Holiness the Dalai Lama if he would consider taking part in writing a book on this topic. The Dalai Lama immediately liked the idea, and readily agreed to be interviewed. Later Rinpoche Lakha honored me by suggesting that I did the interviews and wrote the book.

If there is one man who has applied himself to solving the dilemmas of human existence, it is the Dalai Lama. He is known for his ability to maintain a loving, philosophical overview of people's emotions and behavior and the consequence thereof, and I am deeply honored that His Holiness the Dalai Lama agreed to be part of this book and to follow the subsequent process. In that connection, I would like to point out right away that this book was not produced the same way as the otherwise well-known dialog books with the Dalai Lama. My intention was to combine the knowledge I have gained by working with businesses and people throughout the world with his Buddhist, worldly-wise and philosophical approach to life. The book therefore contains excerpts from my interview with the Dalai Lama, in which he responds to some of the questions that are the foundation for this book.

When writing this book, I began simply by asking questions and gathering stories from all sorts of people. Putting my international business network to practical use I was able to contact hundreds of employees, middle managers and top leaders from all over the world, making sure that people from every level of the traditional company hierarchy were represented.

It soon became apparent that many people are already trying out new approaches. Because independently of trade, culture and nationality there is a general feeling that things have to change, because something about global business market and the global society of today has gone off track.

A thorough examination of existing research revealed that on a global level, work-related ethical dilemmas are very similar. The circumstances and background for the dilemmas obviously differ from country to country, but essentially the ethical dilemmas that present themselves to corporations, to leaders and to employees, are strikingly similar throughout the world – as are their solutions.

OCEAN OF BUDDHIST WISDOM

After careful deliberation and preparation, I flew out to Dharamsala in the northern region of India to meet with His Holiness the Dalai Lama.

Cold winds had swept the Himalayan Mountains for days and there was a slight humidity that made the gusty winds pierce straight through my many layers of clothing. Clouds zipped across the lead grey sky as I crossed the yard between the Tibetan Temple and the small palace where the Dalai Lama resides.

The security check was stricter than ever before in my many years of visiting. The Dalai Lama had recently been declared a target for terrorists, because he had spoken of the injustice in the world. I sipped hot tea in the waiting area and looked at the numerous honorary degrees, distinctions and official gifts the Dalai Lama had received over the past 50 years. Behind me was a big topographical map of Tibet and I wondered about this land, which is basically one big mountain.

Down the hall I heard the voice of the Dalai Lama. In the course of our greeting we quickly reestablished the warm human connection we have so often shared when we had met through my work with the Tibet Charity. It still amazes me how easy it is to be enveloped in his presence. I know the Dalai Lama has a busy schedule, but he still takes all the time we need.

The Dalai Lama is very insightful and, as always keen to gain new knowledge and a new perspective on things. Throughout our conversations, he displayed a remarkable ability to shed new light on the principles of human potential, ethics, leadership, religion and the complexity of the world today. We talked about the strengths and weaknesses of various global, economic systems and of finding meaningfulness in our daily lives and jobs.

My admiration for the Dalai Lama has grown considerably over the course of our conversations. His immense knowledge and humbleness has inspired me – and should indeed inspire everyone – to look deep inside themselves for answers, which are sometimes cloaked, hidden behind the blinds of comfort, materialism or narrow-mindedness. I have never felt as welcome as in the presence of the Dalai Lama. He allowed me to catch a glimpse of the vast ocean of Buddhist wisdom he embodies, and for that I am eternally grateful. But above all, it is the sound of his laughter that I cherish the most.

The corporate world
– The key to radical change

Although this book was written for the individual human being, it is also important to focus specifically on business and work life because many of the inherently negative dynamics of human behavior manifest themselves predominately in this particular aspect of life. Therefore this is also where our future can be changed most fundamentally and most quickly for the better.

If you look at the 100 strongest economies in the world, half of them are private companies (multinationals), and the other half countries. Exxon Mobil's economic capacity for instance, is as strong as Pakistan's. In actual fact these multinationals have more power, and more economic strength to back it up, than many of the democratically elected governments of the world. Decisions are being made taking into consideration profit alone, without adhering to the democratic rules of global collective efforts.

Often the fate of entire countries (and of the people who live there) depend more on decisions made in boardroom meetings in these capitalistic enterprises than on democratic processes and holistic concerns.

The code of knighthood

In the 14th century, the French knight Geoffroi de Charny, a leading spokesman for the moral code of knighthood, decreed, 'The more able should do more'. We don't have to pretend that we are knights, but his message is pure and simple: with great power, wealth and ability comes great responsibility.

We all share responsibility for the world, poor and rich alike. Only the rich naturally have a bigger responsibility, because their wealth gives them a bigger circle of influence. I will return to this idea of a circle of influence and how to utilize it to your full potential.

A small number of individuals literally have the power to change the course of the world radically and to improve the life condition of millions of their fellow human beings. That is a fantastic opportunity to have, and it is a big responsibility to use it well.

However, it is important to realize and acknowledge that everybody's actions make a difference. People with less influence just work on a smaller scale. Their human potential may be as great, or even greater, than that of a successful business owner or a world leader. In other words it is not the scale of your actions that make you ethically responsible, but simply that you make the most difference that you possibly can.

It is all about Love

As humans, we have the mental capacity and spiritual aspiration that enable us to act beyond our instincts. Part of our nature is to reflect on the meaning of life, and, to a large extent, our behavior is determined by this existential search.

Since the beginning of time, differing philosophies and religions have emerged, each represented by spiritually enlightened leaders, who have expounded the true way to reach God. Interestingly, when you filter out the different cultural backgrounds, the essence of all spiritual teachings can be summed up in one word – Love. Love of the earth that supports you, love of your fellow human beings and love of the divine (the God) that inspires you and guides you.

Out of this simple and beautiful universal message have come many varied methods, techniques, practices and ways to reach divine aspiration.

But over time, good principles have been corrupted in the hands of lesser men. Ways to spiritual liberation became rigid laws upheld by ruthless religious regimes whose leaders had forgotten about the love and tolerance taught by the original enlightened ones. Through this, all major religions have turned into dogmas, which basically keep people in a state of fear instead of supporting them in finding their inner potential.

Fear and blind religious faith have developed in us a strong tendency to always stick with what we have got. To never want to change anything, even though we are consciously aware of the flaws and shortcomings of the systems and structures we adhere to. This tendency is extremely dangerous in the light of the world's current state

The answer is to tap into our inner spiritual streak, develop it and collectively reach a higher level of consciousness – the next natural step in human evolution is homo spiritualis.

Survival is on the line.

No need for a spiritual go-between

Nearly every tradition and spiritual practice around the world agrees on the tripartite constitution of the human: mind, body and spirit. We have begun to understand quite a lot about how the brain and body work, but this book will focus on how all human beings must open up to their inner spirituality and literally take responsibility for life itself.

It was once accepted that a few initiated – the so-called spiritual elite – told you what and how to believe. This religious monopoly ensured the priesthood great power and wealth in society. This applied to all religions. To sustain this immense wealth and power, the various religious brands were willing to commit atrocities in the name of God.

But in today's 'global' world, most individuals will soon realize that there is no need for an ordained go-between to connect them with the spiritual realm. This realization is the next natural step in human evolution and will introduce an era where humanity connects directly with the spiritual realm – and draws a straight line between man and his spirituality.

Whether or not the self-proclaimed intermediaries between society and the divine powers were ever profoundly needed is food for thought, but the religious establishment was always characterized by power, wealth and influence. This created a lucrative position for the few elite and a barrier for common people who were prohibited from thinking for themselves – strictly against the intention of the original teachers.

If we look at the development of our own inherent spirituality, we can see that there have been many obstacles. When it comes to religion, many people exercise extreme tolerance and loyalty towards the religious system that has been handed down to them by their parents and grandparents. This makes them extremely reluctant to accept any changes whatsoever. Mental rigidity obviously creates huge hurdles.

What is the recipe for a human being?

What makes up a human being? Is it 20% body, 30% mind, and 50% spirit? Or is it 99% biology and 1% elusive divinity? What are we born with and what do we learn from our environment? What will future evolution of the human species hold in store for us?

Scientists and philosophers have always tried to establish the interconnection between heredity and environment. The paradox is that when we are born we are tabula rasas – blank canvases – but already possess vast biological knowledge. According to leading neurological research, we are born with certain inherent abilities to help us actively absorb from and make sense of the environment.

One of these abilities is to ask ourselves self-reflective existential questions, which enable us to adjust our ethical behavior. Even the physical universe supports this idea. Mankind is finally opening up new doors of perception. We are slowly beginning to explore the vast personal spiritual resources coded in our very own biological foundation.

The consequence of such exploration is, either to leave the ranks of established religion, which in most cases have grown rigid with outdated ceremonies anyway, or to stay and work to revitalize your particular church from the inside out. The worst of all is to do nothing, and just remain a passive member in an effort to cling on to your social status and the acceptance of the congregation.

Ethics are in our genes

There are many different ways to view us as a species, ranging from spiritual beings with a universal ethical purpose to mere primates only here to procreate. It is the overall existential question to which there are many answers, but few that have stood the test of time.

The cultural diversity of mankind can be fascinating and you can sense a second layer of meaning behind the various schisms and dogmas: that behind all the differences was unity. Many observations indicate that, deep down, all known religions and theories tap into the same divine source.

If you could sift all the beliefs, philosophies and scientific schools through a cultural sieve we would have a human divine essence of wisdom. This essence would be the origin of all interpretations and translations. A united wisdom. And through this deeper human wisdom, one could attempt to uncover the ethical 'DNA' of humanity.

This string of human core values will, when fully uncovered, prove that we all share the same inner ethics – beyond any cultural or social differences we might have developed. And at our deepest ethical core lies the unwavering certainty that all humans are equally valuable regardless of our social status, wealth or education.

This book presumes that all human beings are born with a basic ethical foundation; these core values constitute a hidden code, which, despite our superficial differences, reveals the interconnectedness of all humanity. When we realize and globally acknowledge this, it will give us the much-needed perspective on our future actions, and enable us all to tap into our collective awareness, where we will see ourselves as one species – originating from one source.

In other words, ethics are woven into our genes, providing us with a natural and universal understanding of how to conduct ourselves in the world. Embracing both the individual and the collective will ensure a sustainable future for mankind.

Sebastian: Should you hide your religious beliefs in an effort to be accepted?

Dalai Lama: I think that honoring one's religion is an individual matter, but we must learn to respect other people's right to believe in something other than what we believe in ourselves. We must learn to be tolerant.

In one of the Buddhist teachings it is said, 'I will not change my manner of thinking for anything.' I can change my physical appearance and behavior, and still remain true to my original thinking on the inside.

I cannot speak for other traditions, but Buddhism is a way of life. It is a way of thinking and of training your mind, and it has nothing to do with changing the colors of your clothes.

Some of my American friends, who have become followers of Zen, have changed all their clothing to the costume of a Japanese Zen monk. They even changed their furniture in their home to become completely Japanese. That is to go to the extreme.

You don't become a Buddhist because you wear certain clothes or specific items. You practice Buddhism by striving to become humble, honest and tolerant.

There is also a certain Westerner, who has proclaimed himself to be a very high lama from Tibet. When he came to attend my teachings, he would first send some of his students to reserve a seat for him. Then he would come and take his seat, and his students would put a blanket around him, as if he was a high positioned lama (he chuckles).

This makes no sense. Frankly speaking it's quite silly. Anyone who feels that the Buddhist approach is more effective, more suitable to him or her, can practice Buddhism. And there is no need to tell other people. But if another individual shows a real interest in your religion, I think it is good to share your own honest experience with that person.

You should not try to convince them to do the same in his or her life. Just share your own experience, so he or she can then choose what's right for him or her.

As the Dalai Lama mentions, it doesn't suffice to don certain clothes and then insist that one has become more spiritual for that reason. This is not to criticize Buddhism in particular – because this phenomenon to change our external appearance is seen in followers of all religions – but over the past ten years it has – particularly in Western countries – become very fashionable to wear Buddhist prayer beads and use Buddha sculptures and figurines for mere decorative purposes, e.g. as candles or bath mats. Buddhism has become popular to the point where it has become problematic because certain alternative New Age interpretations of Buddhist principles do away with personal human responsibility. Watered-down Buddhist 'explanations' of how everything is exactly the way it should be, how the Universe is self-regulating and how the unfortunate or suffering have caused their own karma, make it convenient and easy to turn a blind eye. Passive acceptance of the state of things is terribly dangerous because it undermines the human feeling of personal responsibility.

Ants are more important than us

*'Stick your finger into a bowl of water.
Then take it out again and measure the circumference of
the hole it leaves behind. That is how irreplaceable you are.'
(Chinese proverb for irreplaceability)*

When looking at the responsibility we have as human beings for today's global challenges and looming disasters, there is no doubt that we have a lot of work cut out for us. Because of us, the planet's ecosystem is facing rather great difficulties. The vast majority of normal functioning organisms try to find a balance with the surrounding ecosystem – as you know, it is not wise to kill the host as that would mean that the ball is over. In fact, if we removed humanity from the face of the Earth, the planet and the ecosystem would only benefit from it.

According to biologist, Edward O. Wilson, we are simply not important to the ecosystem as we do not pollinate, clean or aid any vital processes of any other species. If all ants died out, however, it would be the end of this cycle on Earth and the whole ecosystem would break down and reboot itself. His words ought to make us reconsider the relative importance of humankind.

Whether or not you believe in a higher power is not really relevant to this book's message. What matters is that we all need to reclaim our personal ethical responsibility and act accordingly. The important thing is to find a sustainable way to live in harmony with Earth and its entire species.

Do you realize that if we parked all the cars in the world in one long row they would reach around the world 72 times? A study done by the Center for International Earth Science Information Network at Columbia University and the Wildlife Conservation Society shows that 83% of the global surface is clearly marked by human activity and all of it has been marked by pollution and greenhouse effects. Yet we are almost stupidly reluctant to stop and reconsider our actions. But as globalization catches on we are beginning to realize that we cannot just export our waste or push it aside. Pollution knows no boundaries.

The consciousness of other people's suffering is slowly, but steadily, finding its way through the cracks of our stern mechanisms of denial – and that is cause for hope.

Capitalism version 2.0
– in which we spend our lives longing for things we do not really need

This globe has plenty of resources to ensure good living conditions for everyone. It is the basic formula of distribution, which is at fault. Many people argue that if we utilized all the resources in a sustainable fashion, and redistributed them equally among every citizen of this Earth, there would be more than enough for everyone.

Capitalism has provided amazingly for many individuals and for a few rich countries. It has taught mankind to utilize our competitiveness to the fullest, and even though capitalistic selection has always followed the Darwinian principle of survival of the fittest, capitalism has made possible several quantum leaps. Whether or not we leapt in the right direction remains to be seen.

On the one hand capitalism gave us entrepreneurial drive and made us gather/hunt/develop beyond our basic needs for food and shelter. On the other hand a one-sided focus on materialistic values has evolved into a ferocious greed and over-consumption to such a degree that, absurd as it sounds, many people now literally eat themselves to death.

Capitalism has inspired many wonderful discoveries, and much pivotal scientific and industrial knowledge has emerged as a result of it. But pure capitalism nevertheless embodies a dangerous, mindless drive for more, which, combined with short-sightedness and fear, has taken us too close to the edge.

If we add power without humility to the capitalist equation, we start to recognize our current world order. With such a strong cocktail rushing through our veins, and taking into account our self-centeredness, the results are inevitable.

It does indeed seem unlikely that a global community of sustainability, trust, generosity, compassion and collective consciousness could emerge from the governing principles of capitalism, does it not?

The 'Doomsday Clock' is ticking

So even though our behavior is governed by our life conditions, there is evidence that we are able to transcend to a holistic level of consciousness where 'our needs' no longer control us. To a level where we can act rather than react. Where an inner calm mind will not be disturbed by exterior aspects. A level where egocentric hyper individualism will never overshadow our sense of unity. Where we acknowledge our inner alarm and avoid self-destructive and unethical acts no matter what the conditions are. What would the world look like then?

Fortunately, many people have already realized that we inhabit a planet with a finely balanced ecosystem and live accordingly. Unfortunately the majority does not, and the destruction of the system continues. So our behavior as a species is bewildering from a holistic point of view.

'The Doomsday Clock', which hangs at the University of Chicago, is a symbolic reminder of mankind's dance with destruction. The dials are currently set at 6 minutes to midnight – 6 minutes to Doomsday. Imagine if we had used the entire resources spent on arms race to secure a sustainable future?

Change is good
– Total transformation is better

All alarms are going off and we need to take action now. Produce change now. Discard our old standards and behavior. Make it happen and use our personal circles of influence. For the time to make a difference, to bring about a revolution, is now – by taking personal responsibility for global ethical behavior.

If history has taught us anything, it is that we must always be prepared to change our ways. We must read the signs in our surroundings – the signs of the times – and act upon them. We need to surf the wave of change rather than be swept away by it.

Earlier civilizations arrogantly (or because they simply did not know better) overlooked the warning signs, relying too much on their own capabilities and grandeur. They paid the ultimate price for their arrogance: extinction! The lesson we must learn is humility.

We must be humble in our attitude towards the environment – our very foundation for life – and towards the global family of which we are all a part.

Nature works in cycles – it builds up and breaks down – in repetitious cycles of growth and harvest. This principle, which governs everything else on Earth, includes us too. Things have to die in order for others to blossom.

World Inc. is under severe pressure

With respect to development and change processes in organizations, it has been confirmed over and over that you need to pay attention to two key elements: awareness and timing.

Imagine that you are standing in the wake of the ocean enjoying the gentle waves swirling pleasantly around your feet. It is easy to be lulled into such passive mode that you do not even notice the huge wave heading towards the shore. You realize it too late and are washed under and dragged out to sea.

Even in times when everything is calm we must be aware of our surroundings. Even assuming that you do observe the huge wave heading towards the shore, your timing must be perfect to get onto the wave and ride it. If we are unaware or become too arrogant in our comfort zone, it will kill us.

One of the problems of Western civilization is that growth is always viewed as something good, whereas degeneration (death) is always viewed as something bad. This idea is part of our cultural programming; it has made us stiff and unable to handle real change. Culturally, it makes us exist in a peculiar, defiant opposition to the universe surrounding us, which is in a constant flux.

Today we are in the unique position of actually being able to make a change for the better, because we know the five elements that lead to the downfall of civilization. Now we need 'only' apply the knowledge that has been given to us.

Many elements must work together in harmony if we are to achieve optimal results during a time of change. These elements can be described as follows:

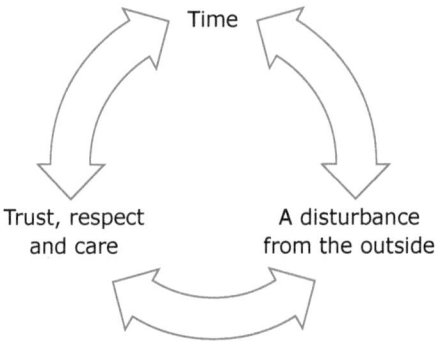

Figure: Elements in the process of change

EQUATION FOR CHANGE

When a company wants advice on how to go through with a new development we typically gather all the information as follows:

- How much pressure is there from the competition and from society?
- How much time do you have to improve your market position?
- How well do the organization's management and employees react to feedback?

If we look at the world as a company in need of consultancy, an experienced business consultant would think twice before taking on this particular job because all three factors in the equation are at critical levels:

- The World Inc. is under severe pressure
- Time is running out
- Feedback-wise the numerous horrendous mistakes in The World Inc.'s past have apparently taught the leadership nothing!

A tsunami wave of change will soon be upon us and The World Inc. is not ready. Environmental issues arise from every corner of the globe. The consequences of capitalistic growth and development are tilting the balance of the planet, and there is a very understandable feeling of injustice and growing unrest among the countless poor.

The only hope for The World Inc. is the fact that we know how to avoid self-destruction and that we have the technological and economic resources available in order to act.

Some transformations slip in and take place unnoticed while others leave our personal world in turmoil. Some are self-initiated while others are imposed on us from the outside. From the research into happiness done by Martin E. P. Seligman we know that having influence over your own life makes you happier, whereas a feeling of being dragged along and having no control over the events in your life is experienced as a negative thing. In other words, if transformation is initiated by yourself, it will be experienced as less painful than a transformation, which is imposed on you.

When a human being clearly understands the deeper meaning in a larger context, nothing can hold him or her back. All opposition, pain and privation will be overcome by meaningfulness. It is in our 'ethical DNA' to transcend the primitive ego and expand our field of consciousness. Holistic consciousness will give us access to our inner realm of meditative balance and make even the most hectic turmoil and transformation seem like gentle ripples on the surface of a calm sea.

As human beings – privately and professionally – we must understand what sort of change we are headed towards and prepare accordingly.

Crossroads

Human beings can attain a worthy and harmonious life only if they are able to rid themselves, within the limits of human nature, of the striving for materialistic fulfillment. The goal is to raise the spiritual values of society.

The examples set by great personages are the only thing that can lead us to do noble deeds and to a truly ethical existence. Money only appeals to selfishness and always irresistibly tempts its owner to abuse it. Can anyone imagine Jesus or Gandhi with stuffed moneybags?

In Western society stress, depression and nervous breakdowns force many people to rethink their way of life. The overwhelming number of books, magazines, CDs with the song of dolphins and TV programs on how to quick-fix your life is a clear indication that many people are struggling tremendously to find their balance and flow. Many have realized that the wonders of flat-screen TVs, cell phones and cars forever being exchanged for newer and better models, do not make us happy. With this realization confusion sets in and everything grinds to a halt. Something is not right in our lives.

You get the same feeling when you realize that a while back, you took the wrong turn at the crossroads. It slowly dawns on you that the landscape does not look the way it should, and that at some stage you will have to pull over to find your bearings, because it makes no sense to keep going in the wrong direction. Of course it is annoying that you have gone the wrong way, but when you realize that the crossroads was a very long way back – in fact it was so far back that it was one of your ancestors who went down the wrong road generations ago – your mind really starts spinning.

It is like a man who, while putting a new roof on his house, realizes that the foundations are just about to slide. Facing an overwhelming task often results in helpless apathy – an acceptance of the state of things – because the individual feels that he is up against impossible odds. But it is precisely from this burning platform that we will change the world.

When everyone comes to terms with the fact that we are all in this together, it will make no sense to focus on the differences in our culture, experience or religion. What does make sense is to search for the fundamental code that binds together all humanity – our common ethics will create a unity from which to go forth, and on which we can make a sustainable future. That future can become a reality through the following four governing principles.

We are one people

Scientific research shows that every living human being on Earth descends from the same basic population. As a species we have one genetic point of origin. According to the so-called displacement model, the same mtDNA (mitochondrial DNA) sequence can be found in every single human being. This means that we all have genetic material from the same woman, who lived 130,000 years ago. Scientific evidence speaks of a tough beginning for our species; the three or four human variations and the type of people we descend from nearly became extinct.

Sixty thousand years ago humans were not coping very well. The last bastion was a small piece of land in East Africa, south of the Sahara. Many scientists believe that we were down to fewer than 10,000 of our forefathers – some even say around 2,500 – at the lowest point of human existence on Earth.

Earth's current population of over six billion people grew from this one small human tribe. This is why even today everybody's DNA is practically identical. Three billion letters that repeat themselves twice throughout our 50 trillion cells constitute the Genetic ACGT code, and yet the genetic differences from one person to another are almost non-existent.

Only a few thousand individuals squeezed through the evolutionary eye of a needle. Think about it – all human beings who live on Earth today descend from these 2,500 individuals. That makes us One People – one tribe – one family.

OVERPOPULATION AND NATURAL MIGRATION

In other words, our current immense differences are not biologically founded, but have emerged from our different environments and cultures. Time and geography have given rise to the cultural and social multitudes of our world today.

Many of our ancestors understood how many individuals could inhabit a certain area of land without depleting the natural resources. So when the tribe grew in numbers some had to emigrate. New lands came to be inhabited because of natural migration – a pattern which has repeated itself over and over for the past 60,000 years right up until today, when human beings reside in even the most remote areas of the world.

In more recent times the pattern of voluntary emigration due to limited resources is practiced on the Pacific island of Tikopia, where the island's population never exceeds 1,100. When that number is exceeded, some of the inhabitants have to sail off and find a new place to live, for the greater benefit of the entire society, and to maintain the fragile ecological balance of the island. This custom may seem cynical, but it has enabled the stable and sustainable existence of the tiny island society.

Do we have, then, a human instinct, which regulates the given number of individuals in a social group? If we do, then where did we go wrong globally? In certain areas of the world we have certainly exceeded that number. In the year 2007 half of the world's population was crowded together in cities, as opposed to living in the countryside.

We face the huge challenge of overcoming the dilemma of mega-cities, the world's urban equivalent to black holes in space that swallow all matter around them. When the gravity of darkness becomes sufficiently intense, it tends to suck in all life from its surroundings. And these condensed cities do seem to pull everything down into eternal darkness with an insatiable appetite. Within the megacities, mankind's herd mentality has spun out of control and left us immensely vulnerable to poverty, social degradation and pandemonium.

Are we programmed for cultural diversity?

In the light of historical development it is interesting to reflect on what would have become of the human race if we had stayed together in one big herd. Would we even exist today? Or have we survived and conquered the world exactly because of our tendency for natural migration, which again has led our evolution towards cultural multiplicity?

When we travel around the world today and meet Inuit, Indians, Arabs, Japanese, Africans and so on, it is obvious that our cultures, traditions and experience have diversified immensely.

But our origin is one tiny herd, which over thousands of years has managed to spread itself all over the world. The human races are in fact one race colored by the environment in which our ancestors happened to end up. With this new knowledge, it no longer makes sense to uphold old-fashioned boundaries between people.

According to our DNA we are one people – interrelated – and it is about time we acted like it. Most cultures consider unselfish compassion a noble human trait that everyone should try to practice. In most cultures, it is taken for granted that you always help your own family. So really, the only thing new about this book is that it urges you to, instead of limiting your altruistic practice to people of your own culture, or to people to whom you are closely related, extend your natural human capacity for compassion to everyone you meet. We are all related.

We need to take care of the entire family – the big herd – all 6,691 billion of them. And we cannot apply different rules to different locations or races – we are one big herd.

Sadly, most of us in the West are completely preoccupied with stuffing ourselves and hoarding as much treasure as we possibly can. And that is dangerous, because there is a basic human ethical congruity between all humans that cannot be meddled with without causing harm to ourselves.

When fear pushes us towards the unethical, something inside us shrivels up and dies. This process needs to stop. Right here, right now, with the help of every living human being.

As appears in the following, the Dalai Lama believes that if you possess more than you need for yourself and your closest family's foreseeable future, you are greedy. Does that apply to you?

And what would the world look like if children in every school around the world were taught how to avoid greed, maybe for just one hour a week throughout their education?

You could say, 'You make a living with what you get. You make a life with what you give.'

Sebastian: How do you make sure never to become greedy when you start making money?

The Dalai Lama (laughs): Well, it makes sense to financially secure yourself and your family's existence for the foreseeable future. A basic foundation for life, for survival and for a reasonably happy future.

I honestly don't think that anything beyond that is necessary.

But one side of your mind might still want more, although more is strictly not necessary. A lot of people seem to always say 'I want, I want' ... and that is greed.

It is wise for someone who progresses materially to make sure that a larger circle of his or her community also benefits. His or her desire to accumulate more should be done reasonably and they should be sensible to a greater good.

As you progress in the field of material things you need to use common sense to avoid becoming greedy.

Because if you think carefully, reflect carefully on the matter, you will see that the more you have – the greedier you become.

In the end the only sense of satisfaction you will have is material. This leads to suffering.

History – something that you can learn from

*"Sometimes, by chance, history opens
a unique window into the future."*
(Voltaire)

Yes, the challenges seem overwhelming but we have the technology to observe, analyze and understand our circumstances. We can find out what is happening on the other side of the globe in a split second, and that actually gives us a unique set of information to navigate from – to act upon. Furthermore, we are the first civilization on Earth to have a real opportunity to make use of our knowledge of past civilizations and their downfall.

We know what happened to the Mayans, the early Easter Islanders, the ancient Egyptians, the Romans and the Greeks. It is all in the history books.

There are two main differences between those ancient civilizations and ours: they had no real communication between their societies, hence little or no knowledge of each other's history and experiences; and our stakes are much higher, because our downfall will be on a global scale.

When prompted, we sense the unfairness of the global set-up on an almost instinctive ethical level. But what are the actual warning signs? It is not like we don't know what to for look for. Jared Diamond, Professor in history, and evolutionary biologist, points to several factors that can signify the impending downfall of a culture:

- Destruction of the environment
- Changes in the climate
- War
- Dysfunctional trade
- Inability to make structural change in society

Any of those sound familiar? So we do have a good idea of which issues we need to address to put the course of human existence back on track, globally.

Ancient societies did not have these factors well documented and available for study, and paid the ultimate price: the collapse of their entire culture.

We know the historical and statistical facts, we know what is going on and we have the power and wealth to mend our ways – all the warning signs are flashing for our globe and for our species.

When we look carefully at the current state of things on our Earth from the perspective of Jared Diamond's factors, it is no wonder that our internal instinct alarms are going off like crazy. Some scientists estimate that we have less than ten years to right the wrongs, or the damage will be irreversible.

Søren Kierkegaard, the Danish existentialist philosopher said, 'The captain on the bridge of a ship heading straight for the rock has a certain amount of time in which he can decide what action to take. After that, the rock decides.' Such is the nature of irreversibility.

THE OSTRICH ATTITUDE

In the long run, it always costs more to repress new knowledge than to adapt to it. We may have many 'good' reasons not to adapt and process the information we have. It may be too painful, too shocking or too demanding to change our current model of the world. And so we end up not dealing with it – at least for a while. Nevertheless, experience has also shown that however much we digress or let ourselves be mind-numbed by entertainment or consumption; we cannot escape our instinctive feeling of alarm.

How did it come to this?

Man's inflated view of himself may have put him in this precarious situation. It would not be the first time in history we have boosted our human egos while hanging ourselves out to dry. Aristotle in his Scala Naturae puts man on the very peak of the evolutionary step ladder, and Christianity states that: 'As man is created in the image of God, so animals and all creatures of the world are created for man as our servants.' As far as Darwin was concerned, man retained his number one spot as the peak of evolution, but today scientists believe that the great apes are a separate species, which continue to develop.

As opposed to Darwin and Aristotle, today's science would have never put man on the throne of evolution. Any species is always on the very peak of its own evolution. Contemporary biologists have now realized that we are in fact just one species among many, all of whom are under continued evolutionary development and change. Which means we share our throne with representatives of every other species.

Considering that these other species, due to human activities, have perished at a rate unlike any other since the distinction of dinosaurs 65 million years ago, we should beg humble forgiveness from all the other species on this Earth and excuse ourselves with the fact that we simply did not know any better. That we had been told over and over that we were the supreme beings on Earth and that that gave us a somewhat twisted view on reality.

But today, that is no longer a valid excuse. Today, we are well aware of what we are doing. As far as we know, we are the only species that possesses the ability to think in abstract, the foundation for spirituality – we are definitely not able to communicate with others who are. We can reflect metaphysically and existentially, and with this ability comes a responsibility for all life on Earth.

When we take our abilities into account, man is the species with the highest developed transformation potential. When it comes to our inherent skills, there is practically no limit to what we can become. It is 'merely' a matter of daring to believe it – and to translate the belief into action. If we wish to act as God, we have to take divine responsibility for our actions as well.

Absurd juxtapositions

We in the West are stuffing ourselves in pure desperation. That is why our healthcare system is tremendously overloaded from the flood of diseases of affluence: obesity, type 2-diabetes, coronary heart disease ... the list is long. And it is not only our bodies that are suffering, but also our mental health. Alcoholism, depression, and a range of other psychiatric illnesses are on the rise.

Today obese children outnumber malnourished ones according to WHO's Obesity Taskforce. Think about it.

We have an obesity epidemic on our hands, yet the majority of Earth's population lives below the poverty threshold and thousands of human beings die every single hour of extreme malnutrition. After thousands of years of civilization, the differences between rich and poor are still absurd.

In many places in the world athletes, pop musicians and movie stars literally make millions of dollars a week, while just around the corner an entire family tries to get by on a couple of dollars, or less, each day.

The richest 400's wealth is equal to the 3,7 billion poorest ...

Today, the 400 richest people own more than the poorest half of the Earth's population.

History – something that you can learn from

The richest people in the world 2010

	Name	Net Worth (US$)	Citizenship	Source
1	Carlos Slim Helú	53.5 bilion	Mexico	Telmex, América Móvil, Grupo Carso
2	Bill (William H.) Gates III	53.0 bilion	USA	Microsoft
3	Warren Buffett	47.0 bilion	USA	Berkshire Hathaway, Inv.
4	Mukesh Ambani	29.0 bilion	France	Reliance Industries
5	Lakshmi Mittal	28.7 bilion	India	Arcelor Mittal
6	Lawrence Ellison	28.0 bilion	USA	Oracle
7	Bernard Arnault	27.5 bilion	France	LVMH
8	Eike Batista	27.0 bilion	Brazil	Mining, Oil
9	Amancio Ortega	25.0 bilion	Spain	Zara Clothing
10	Karl Albrecht	23.5 bilion	Germany	Aldi

(Source: Forbes list of the World's Billionaires at www.forbes.com. The list currently changes quickly due to the turbulent world economy.)

Alarmingly, this imbalance increases every day. Particularly now when the global recession makes the rich world amass bank packages and rescue plans. Don't get me wrong – something needs to be done about the immediate economic situation – but surely not at the cost of the world's poorest. 1.3 billion human beings live on less than 1 US dollar a day in extreme poverty, as defined by the World Bank. If we increase that amount to 2 US dollars a day, that number is 3 billion human beings In comparison, every EU cow is subsidized with more than 2.5 US dollars each day.

Reading the 'UN Human Development Report', we find that 54 poor countries are now even poorer than in 1990, in spite of the general economic growth in the world and despite the UN's aim to cut the world's poverty in half by 2015. Economic growth in East and South Asia has released up to 200 million people from the grip of poverty, but at the same time Sub-Saharan Africa has become increasingly poorer.

Over three billion human beings are born, live and die in poverty. But as it happens, millions of them would not have to be poor if, for instance, the ten richest people decided to redistribute a little of their wealth.

If we add up these people's fortunes, we get a total of a little more than 342,000,000,000 US dollars and if each of these immensely rich people took 1 billion US dollars for themselves and their closest relatives, wouldn't it be safe to say that they would all be reasonably assured for the future? That would leave 332,000,000,000 US dollars for distribution amongst the world's poorest – and if the daily ration were increased to 3 US dollars to cover the increase of cost of food, this would mean that for 10 years more than 30 million human beings would be lifted out of poverty! Ten rich people – such an impact on humanity – thought provoking.

Several of these ten unbelievably rich people already give quite a bit – some of them – like Bill Gates and Warren Buffett and 34 others for example – have given half of their fortune to charity. But then imagine if we all took generosity one step further and reallocated our surplus to those in need of a sustainable future.

And yes, I realize that you cannot construct it quite as simply as that – and to merely show that you are donating money could result in those receiving the funds are made passive and thus locked in their receiving position. One idea could be to create a foundation that – free of national political interests, religious restrictions or inherited cultural limitations – could be responsible for a total redistribution – and that is exactly the great idea behind the OneGlobeOnePeople Foundation. And there is a lot of work to be done, because at the moment about half of those children who are born in the poorest countries in the world die before they turn five and 1/3 of the population in third world countries do not reach the age of 40, whereas each year, NATO spends 456 billion US dollars on military hardware. And no – you cannot construct it like that – or is that not exactly what you can if you are an ethical human being?

Here is the math: A total fortune of 426,000,000,000 US dollars/ – 1,000,000,000 for each of those individuals / for ten years or 3650 days / with 3 US dollars per person per day = 37.990,867 US dollars.

WE SEE WHAT WE BELIEVE WE SEE
... NOT WHAT IS

No matter what we tell ourselves, how steadfast we are in our opinion; history has shown us that it is wise not to burn all your bridges. Our consciousness is, in other words, affected by our environment – our historical and cultural context – which again determines our perception of the world and indeed colors our entire understanding of the relationship between cause and effect.

To see what is behind the symptoms, we sometimes need to look behind the curtains of what we take for granted in our existence and examine the way we interact with the world, our work and with other human beings. It is mind-boggling that many people never reevaluate their perception of life. No matter what they go through. It seems as if they feel it is safer to live their entire life without service checks or upgrades on reality. The most extreme examples of an outlook on life set in stone that I have experienced have been within religious doctrines that paradoxically seem impenetrable where logic and compassion for the society in which they exist are concerned.

For example, when the Catholic faith cannot seem to acknowledge nor act on the AIDS situation or overpopulation, or when extreme fundamentalist Islamic groups issue fatwa after fatwa against people who allegedly disobey the Holy Scriptures, or when they continue to mutilate young girls with crude circumcisions and to consider women lesser beings...

The original founders of the major religions attempted to show humankind the path towards perfection, compassion and emancipation. But it seems their followers over time have lost the essence of the original teachings and now follow only the rituals.

In the Hindu Holy Scripture Bhagavad Gita Lord Krishna proclaims: 'Four castes are created by me according to their qualities and actions.' But in practice, this principle was distorted and birth (family lineage) came to be considered the criterion of caste. As a result, injustices, inequalities, atrocities and terrorization prevailed in the name of religion through history; and are still occurring today.

Buddha emphasized the importance of wisdom, enlightenment and compassion. But many followers were more interested in worldly wisdom and started collaborating with rulers and rich people in order to amass wealth in the name of institutions, stupas (Buddhist shrines) and temples.

The founder of the Jain belief, Mahaveera, taught the importance of non-violence. Followers exhibited their devotion to the Guru by preserving the life of germs in the air, ants on the ground etc. in ritualistic fashion; for instance, Jain followers do not cultivate land, as it is impossible for farmers to avoid hurting living beings.

Jesus proclaimed that passing a camel through the eye of a needle would be easier than the passage of wealthy people to Heaven. If only Christians around the world had heeded these teachings, the Earth would be a different place.

The Prophet Mohammed banned interest on credit. Furthermore he laid down laws for the continuous redistribution of wealth for the benefit of the poor (exactly what we need to do today on a global scale). But today a small minority of Muslims lives in extreme luxury while the vast majority of Muslims in the world are in abject poverty and misery.

The original wisdom of the enlightened ones served a beneficial purpose to humanity as such, but in the hands of lesser men it has been twisted and turned to serve personal gain.

It is difficult to cure voluntary blindness in a human being who refuses to reflect on life, and lives only to uphold the distorted religious laws dictated by the written doctrines of ancient times.

Are we a self-destructive species?

The world today bears witness to many destructive conflicts caused by mental petrifaction. We see incidents so terrifying that we can hardly fathom them: genocide in Darfur, Rwanda and Bosnia, the Chinese government's ongoing violation of human rights, American soldiers' shameful abuse of Iraqi prisoners, mass executions in North Korea – the list of human atrocities and primitive behavior seems endless. And these are only a few blatantly obvious examples taken from violent and armed conflicts around the world.

But if we look at global business life, we see just as many examples of inhuman treatment of people. For example, when Western clothing brands quietly condone the horrendous slave-like conditions of Asian workers. Or when ships are sent to India to be disassembled in makeshift shipyards with no regard for safety, environment or human life.

Every time we watch the news we are confronted by another atrocity, and we must ask ourselves what psychological mechanisms are at work in these people that they are capable of inflicting so much suffering on their fellow human beings?

This entire book is built on the belief that we are not inherently a self-destructive species. Human history does much to prove otherwise, but I find it incredibly difficult to believe that mankind, who displays such incredible potential, was constructed simply to destroy itself. Whether or not you believe that life has a purpose, it makes no sense.

Aspects, such as the distribution of wealth, globalization and our interconnectedness must be reconsidered if we are to escape unscathed. It is vital for us to relate to our past.

On a larger scale

With the wave of globalization, the old (economic) paradigm of growth continues on an even larger scale.

Companies are relocating their production to countries with a low-wage workforce in their perpetual chase for even larger profits. The wealthy part of the world has succeeded in finding a method of legally exporting the heaviest, most polluting and backbreaking work processes to poorer countries that have yet to formulate and enforce laws on work environment and environmental issues.

Such irresponsibility increases the polarization between the rich and the poor countries – leaving the poorer even further behind. Powerlessness amongst people in the poorer countries is spreading like cancer, fertilizing the ground for desperate acts. The feeling of being incapacitated – the feeling of helplessness – gives rise to desperation, and we are only too aware of the obvious outlets: religious fundamentalism, terror and destructive conflicts between populations in which the price of human life is low.

We do know in the Western world, that the real cause for these acts of desperation runs deeper than can be solved by sporadic aid to suffering populations or by smoking out the terrorists and dishing out random punishment. Unfortunately, the earlier mentioned apathetic attitude has taken over. It seems as if most people have abandoned all hope of changing the parameters that cause inequality in the world. The obvious solution to our unbalanced and dysfunctional world order lies in the redistribution of the world's wealth and resources.

Sebastian: Why do the majority of people as well as our political leaders continue to believe that capitalistic eco-

nomic growth is the only foundation for prosperity? And what about the unbalanced distribution of the world's resources?

Dalai Lama: This is a key aspect for humanity to solve. Socialism was supposed to take equality into serious consideration. Equal distribution of resources and equal income.

Therefore I have always preferred the socialist idea, but the system or the model itself cannot bring a definite answer or solution – it has to do with the people who control the system and their level of consciousness.

Of course I have always contemplated the gap between rich and poor. It exists on a local level, a national level – the gap between people is very pronounced for instance in India, America and lately also in China. But it also exists on a global level, because the gaps between countries are huge.

From my point of view the gaps are not only ethically wrong; they are the source of many desperate actions. We have to address this problem together and take it very seriously.

Sebastian: Do you agree that we have to come up with another method to distribute the world's wealth if we want to create a sustainable solution?

Dalai Lama: Yes. Centralized unions like China are not the answer. The free market is better, even though it too has its downsides. I have learned that in some countries in Europe the middle-class people are the big majority and the gap between rich and poor is not so large, and that there are very few billionaires. If this is true, then that is certainly better than the gap here in India.

Sebastian: I believe it is due to the tax system. In some countries it is set up in such a way that it is very hard to become extremely rich, as it is to become extremely poor.

Dalai Lama: Well, that is the way they do it then. Taxation can prevent the huge gap in wealth. And all people in the country share some of the growth of the wealthy families or companies.

During my visits to America I have, on a number of occasions, expressed the need to reduce the gap between rich and poor. If we don't, it can lead the poor into deep frustration, which will create hate and finally turn the two sides against each other. This leads to conflicts and, I'm sad to say, violence, and that is never a good way to deal with anything.

Sebastian: I have often said to those I teach that if you are poor you must work honestly and hard to change your circumstances and if you are rich you must work honestly and hard to help others to change their circumstances.

Dalai Lama: That is a very good way of saying it.

We do have the necessary resources

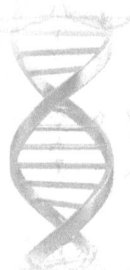

'Only a person who risks is free.'
(Hugo Prather)

Researchers have uncovered many mysteries of the human mind over the last half-century. Scans of the activity of the brain indicate that human beings have mental resources way beyond those we actively use.

Exactly how much of the human brain lies dormant is difficult to say. Nevertheless, people who suddenly gain a new perspective on life are often able to pull out the most incredible resources.

The following is not only based on science and brain research, but also on my own experiences with people going through change. There is no doubt in my mind that we – for various reasons – are kept from realizing our full potential. I have known enough people to experience explosion-like epiphanies to be sure that their talent was always there. It just had to be activated.

A skill must be practiced over and over, and it can often take a long time and a lot of hard work to fully acquire a new skill. Whereas mastering an inner talent often comes quite easily – as soon as you allow yourself to incorporate that talent in your personal identity.

The windblown trees of the west coast

The term 'overshadowed' can be used to signify a person who has a strong innate talent without being aware of it. The moon is a great metaphor for this. We all know that the moon is always there and is always round. It is only when the Earth is blocking the light from the sun that the moon appears to be less than full in the sky. Sometimes the moon is entirely blocked from our vision, but it is still there.

Human potential – your inner core of unused talent(s) – is always there, but can easily be overshadowed by your upbringing or your current life situation. A new perspective, however, can deepen your self-awareness and thereby change your life forever. Most people use only a tiny part of their biological potential.

None of us get through childhood unscathed by negative learning experiences. Think about the physical talent overshadowed, lost, when a child is always the last one to be picked for the team in gym class? The child ends up thinking that he or she is completely useless each time when two team captains try to avoid having a certain boy or girl on their team. If only the teacher had had enough insight to realize what such public humiliation does to a child's fragile psyche and which consequences this 'ritual' can have far into life as an adult.

Overshadowing and environmental conditioning is common in nature. On the northwest coast of Denmark where I grew up, the trees serve as a symbolic reminder of heredity and the environment; they are all contorted – blown inland – by the relentless western wind from the sea. If a similar tree had been planted in less windy conditions – or where the wind blew from alternating directions – would it be straighter and perhaps taller? Of course it would!

Even if you are highly programmed and brainwashed you will – as opposed to the windblown tree – always have an opportunity to free yourself of your past and to shape your own future.

You too would have been another person if you had grown up in a different environment. According to psychological research, we are most receptive in our first four years of life. This is the phase in a human life when we take in the environment completely unfiltered and it is immensely important for our later perception of life.

> *And a woman who held her child closely, said, 'Speak to us about children.' And he answered, 'Your children are not your children. They are the sons and daughters of Life's longing for itself. They come through you but not from you, and though they are with you, yet they belong not to you. You may give them your love but not your thoughts. For they have their own thoughts. You may house their bodies but not their souls, for their souls dwell in the house of tomorrow, which you cannot visit, not even in your dreams. You may strive to be like them, but seek not to make them like you. For life goes not backward nor tarries with yesterday. You are the bows from which your children as living arrows are sent forth. The archer sees the mark upon the path of the infinite, and He bends you with His might that His arrows may go swift and far. Let your bending in the archer's hand be for gladness; for even as He loves the arrow that flies, so He loves also the bow that is stable.'*
> (Khalil Gibran in The Prophet)

Could it be phrased more beautifully? The child as the arrow and its parents as the bow. The function of the parents is to set the arrow in motion – give it enough velocity – not to determine its precise direction or goal. In my way of thinking this is a beautiful and challenging ideal for all parents to consider.

Unlike the windblown trees rooted in the sandy coastal ground, humans can quite easily move to shelter from the wind. In fact we can all reach our full height very quickly given the right circumstances – we need only to free ourselves from our mental blocks.

We are told different stories

We enter life with a wealth of human potential. Some of us are lucky enough to be supported in developing these talents – others are not. The lives we come to live are largely determined by the stories we are told in our childhood. You can only become your true self when you gain awareness of how these narratives have culturally programmed you.

Human consciousness is shaped dramatically during the first few years and to a lesser degree up until ages 6-7. Most of our values and perceptions are laid down in this phase and will continue to influence us and be the foundation for our decisions and opinions – good and bad – later on in life. If one grows up in a culture where all peers believe in reincarnation, or God, or anything, one would naturally come to share that particular belief.

If a person really believes in reincarnation, and lives accordingly, he or she will not be prone to lie, steal or cheat because such acts would negatively influence his or her karma – something that he or she must avoid at all costs, since negative karma comes back to you in the form of tangible disadvantages in your next life. It is a whole different story for someone who grows up in our Western society where competing and getting ahead, often at the cost of others, is often greatly admired in society, where earthly wealth equals human success.

Think of all the female talent wasted over all these years. All the ingenious ideas that never came to fruition, because so many women are systematically being mentally crippled by their environment and shackled by our male-dominated society's conditioning.

Within certain religious societies women have to wear scarves and cover themselves up, allegedly not to tempt the men they encounter. I wonder why these men cannot just control their primitive urges, instead of placing the responsibility with the women? Obviously it is not about the piece of cloth, but about the purpose it serves. If a scarf is worn to protect the skin from sun or dust it has a physical function, but if degradation and low social status is woven into its fabric, it becomes an incredibly heavy and inhibiting accessory.

Sebastian: Why do you think that there are so few women in leading positions in the world?

Dalai Lama: We still have an ancient way of thinking. In ancient times you had to rely on physical strength, and because the male physiology was generally stronger, males took the leading role. I believe that this is the main reason why males became so dominant.

In modern society brain is more important than muscles. And we need to change the perception in society that male individuals should always assume the leadership.

I am not saying that male leaders have bad intentions towards women, but many take their leadership for granted.

Now, the level of consciousness has risen. Through education and the work for women's rights we are on our way to equality. Some feminists even feel that it is time for the women to dominate the men, but that is to take it to the other extreme.

Sebastian: I believe in total equality for all people disregarding color, religion, gender or age. A second injustice cannot be justified by the first. We cannot undo the mistakes of the past, but we can learn from them.

Dalai Lama: A good way to say it – one injustice cannot be undone or balanced by another. It becomes just another injustice.

The most important aspect in the matter of equality between man and woman is that the unbalance is based on a psychological foundation. If the culture favors one gender over another, it will have a profound impact on people's lives.

Most cultures have always favored males, but not all. Someone once told me that on one small island in the Pacific it was the tradition that the women were the leaders of the tribe.

We have to work to educate the cultures that favor one gender over another. Women and men should be treated equally. It is important that the female side also makes an effort. Dialogue must never be conducted with a sense of hostility, but should come from a holistic point of view – regardless of gender – or as you said, regardless of color, religion or age. Through education we can achieve this goal. It will take time because gender discrimination is very integrated in our behavior through ancient social systems and habits. We must give women all the encouragement and support we can.

There is also the matter of differences in religion. On many occasions I have expressed the opinion that there is discrimination between Christians, Muslims, Hindus and Buddhists. It seems to me that women, in general, have more respect for other people's right to believe something other than they do. Here men should learn from the women.

When I give talks in the Himalayan regions, I have noticed more and more women among my audience. The men say that they have other things to do that are more important, but I think that they have false confi-

dence in themselves in thinking that they don't need religion. Everybody needs spirituality, even those who think they don't. In that respect it seems that women, even though it might seem discriminating of me to say so, from a biological standpoint, may have a tendency to understand that better than men. But it needs more research.

On a few occasions I have said this to the Tibetans, and especially to the Tibetan monks, who are against females taking vows to the highest ordination of Buddhism – and I know that there are still some monks who find it very difficult to accept that the times are changing.

A good thing is that many men don't feel that they are more important than women. They have learned to control their aggression and maybe therefore they can show women the same respect they show towards each other. Male chauvinism is a psychological matter and it has taken a stronghold in many societies and cultures. It will take time to alter that perception. But as I mentioned earlier, women seem more interested in faith or religion, and that is also the case with Buddhism.

At the time of the Buddha, Indian society was even more male-oriented than it is today. Even under those circumstances the Buddha gave equality to male and female when it came to the highest ordination. That is very different from other traditions.

I know that it is also mentioned in the scriptures that the monks should be sitting closer to Buddha and the females next in line, but maybe that was how it had to be at that time. Even under those circumstances within a totally male-dominated society in ancient India, the Buddha essentially treated men and women equally. And today in the 21st Century there is a worldwide movement against gender discrimination and in support of equality.

We within Tibetan Buddhism must revive the highest ordination for Buddhist nuns. On occasion I have expressed this, not to everybody's liking, but as a leader you cannot be liked by everyone all the time.

But we have moved ahead as far as we can to promote studies for women also. In the last 40 years we have introduced the same level of studies in our nunneries as in our monasteries. But with regard to the highest ordination, we also have to consider other Buddhist traditions, like the Thai, the Zen and so forth and we have to do this all together.

But within our Tibetan tradition, as far as knowledge is concerned, we are implementing this way of thinking. We really make an effort to create equality in all matters.

The rigid mind

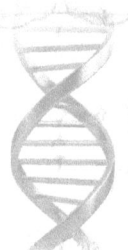

'The only darkness is ignorance.'
(Shakespeare, Twelfth Night)

Mental inflexibility does indeed weigh heavily upon us. Change and renewal is often met with fierce opposition – even today. If the security of the present is removed before you have established trust in the future, you will have conflict.

But it is essential to understand that the soul can set itself free in a split second. We have unlimited access to all our human potential and therefore also to a holistic level of awareness. Maybe this access to an ever-present and eternal field of energy is what we have come to call God?

Once, the Nordic people believed that lightning was Thor the Thunder God going for a ride in his chariot. The Egyptians packed food in with their dead so they would not starve in the next life. Mankind believed that the world was flat, and if you declared that it was 'round' you could be burned for heresy.

If one applies the metaphor of the contorted tree to static religions, it explains much of the hardship we have brought on ourselves over the centuries. The difference between the tree and us is that we can change our individual perception of the world in a split second and thus change everything around us.

THE LOTTERY OF LIFE – WHAT DID YOU GET?

The systems and mechanisms which determine the lives of people all over the world today are not 'fair'. For instance, the fact that different people in different places of the world are born into such extremely diverse circumstances seems very unfair.

One could thus compare the current world order, to a lottery. Your wealth, the resources you are given, as well as your opportunities in life are determined by where and when you are born. Your talents are not a criterion for your personal future and give you no rights as such. Even those of us who were lucky to have been born in a wealthy country, must realize how such an absurd system will naturally generate a massive feeling of unfairness.

On my travels throughout the world, I have often been asked whether I think it is fair that some have so much and some so extremely little. The only answer is: 'No, it is not fair', nor is it logical or right by any measure of human consciousness. Likewise, the problem with the principle of karma is that it is too easy to write off people's suffering simply as karmic punishment for their previous lives. As if they deserved it!

With what kind of fairness then are the lottery tickets of life distributed, and who can change the conditions? This is a question I have asked many wise and learned people. In return, I have been given many elaborate explanations for the situation – what determines your 'ticket' – but remarkably few ideas on how to change the situation.

Religious or spiritual explanations often speak of some sort of reward system or of Karma. 'Everybody must go through their lot in life and live out their Karma', they say. But I must admit that personally I can hardly stand that approach to life any longer. After everything I have seen, such phrases sound hollow, even in my semi-Buddhist heart. Because I know they breed a passiveness – a quiet and stale acceptance – of your lot in life that makes people suffer in silence. In my experience, Karma is often used as an excuse to avoid responsibility.

A friend of mine was traveling in India and she was invited for dinner at a fellow doctor's house. The dinner was beautiful and there was plenty for the few guests at the table. In the courtyard behind the house lived a beggar family. My friend, coming from Western Europe, politely suggested that the remains of the dinner should be taken to the poor family rather than be thrown out. The host was shocked and said, 'No it is their karma and they have to live it. We do not interfere.'

She looked at him calmly and said, 'If that is so they will sit here at this table in the next life and you will sit in the courtyard.' She was never invited back.

Politeness might urge you to hold back, but as an ethical human being you must actively use your indignation to push for positive change in other people's life conditions – karma or no karma.

Waking up to reality

I remember my first personal encounter with deep human despair. It happened back in 2002 on my first trip to Nepal where I was traveling as a Tibet Charity representative, visiting our activities in that area. I had never traveled in the East before, since my area of expertise and my work had been centered on Europe, the USA and Australia, which, despite all their differences, are cultures founded on similar values of democracy, freedom of speech and capitalistic enterprise.

I must admit that the East shocked me. Coming across countless sick and extremely poor people, I was immediately overpowered by despair. I felt engulfed by an endless sea of human suffering. I wanted to help all these people – each and every one of them – right there and then. But there was no way I could. I had been raised in the safe and comfortable environment of Denmark – at that time one of the most socially aware countries in the world, generous with its foreign aid – and my personal encounter with all these sick, despairing and ragged people living in extreme poverty literally took my breath away.

I felt unable to comprehend what my senses were telling me – like the native Indians watching Columbus' ships approaching the shore. They could not comprehend what they were seeing, because they had never seen anything like it before. The difference was of course that I had seen all these suffering, hungry people before – in the papers and on TV. But like so many others from the Western world, I had cleverly managed to repress the reality of those images.

However, standing amidst these people with the smells of sickness, poverty and with the eerie presence of yearlong helplessness creeping through my every pore, my defenses simply crumbled, and I could no longer deny nor repress the shocking facts.

I had recently been elected Vice Chairman for the Tibet Charity and this being my first visit, I knew that I simply had to familiarize myself with the real state of things. I could not budge – and I didn't – but I knew I would be taken way out of my comfort zone in order to process this knowledge. I visited the reception center for Tibetan refugees, which, upon their arrival, takes care of the many refugees who risk a hazardous escape through the Himalayan Mountains. The refugees whom I met there had managed not only to avoid being caught by the ever-present Chinese border patrols, but had also navigated the unforgiving icy mountains – an extreme test of human endurance and psyche.

Many of them had fled and traveled on foot over the world's highest mountain peaks wearing only sandals or canvas sneakers. Quite often, when their shoes or sandals were removed, one or two blackened toes fell off – like sad little lumps of coal.

I met the weary eyes of little kids who had watched their mom or dad collapse and die on the journey through the mountains, and the legless old beggar on his makeshift rolling board

– a sad relative of the brightly colored skateboards that children in the Western world ride around on. Everywhere were children who needed food, care, proper stimulation and parental love. I walked the streets like a zombie. The strong stench of garbage made me nauseous and forced me to stop and take in deep breaths of air that only made me feel even worse. I was Dante in an inferno of human suffering, degradation and helplessness.

One Tibetan woman made an especially big impression on me. I met her during a visit to a health clinic where the Tibet Charity had several volunteers working. I was there to see how the Tibet Charity could increase our help. I had been observing the work in the clinic for a couple of hours when she showed up. She had great difficulty walking, and despite the immense heat, she wore a big scarf, which covered her entire face, except for her eyes. She obviously found it very difficult to maneuver herself around between the many examination beds. I got up and offered her my arm for support. She looked at me through the scarf's small opening for the eyes with deep gratitude, as if I had just offered her something very precious. I helped her to the nearest examination bed and the Tibet Charity health counselor asked me if I would lend a hand with this woman, who had come for her weekly pain relief treatment.

Hesitantly I agreed, while mumbling a few vague sentences about my lack of medical training. She was there for her acupuncture treatment. After the needles were put in and smeared with moxar (a mix of oil and healing herbs), the moxar substance was lit on fire and started smoldering. The heat enhances the pain relief via the acupunctural points, but when there are a lot of burning needles – as was the case with this woman – you need someone to keep an eye on the process. Especially in the case of this woman, whose skin had lost most of its sensitivity due to a serious burn injury, so she might easily be burned even more without noticing it straight away.

When the woman was asked if it was okay that I helped out, she said yes with the same intensity and gratitude as before. Behind a curtain, which created an illusion of privacy, she slowly undressed down to a thin veil over her underwear. The severe burn had disfigured most of her body and face. Once the needles had been placed and set on fire, I was left alone with this woman. Even though the sounds from the health clinic spoke of the world around us, it was as if we were on our own private island. She was on her side, looking at me. I was sitting there smiling the best I could – a somewhat cramped smile I imagine, because I had practically slapped it over my scared face. I wanted to cope with this experience even though I found it difficult – I mean she was the one having to endure a life of what must have been excruciating pain. She looked at me with a pleasant smile and I realized that she was helping me. I wiped the tiny beads of sweat from her face. They quickly reappeared. I realized that I was holding her hand. I felt set free from time and space, and my initial fear and discomfort was gone as I held her scarred hand. She smiled at me and intuitively I reached out and gently stroked her cheek as one would when putting a child down to sleep after a long day. Her skin was like the surface of the moon. They told me that I sat with her for 45 minutes, but I had no conception of time, only our relation of due care existed for me.

Before leaving the clinic she took my hand and squeezed it softly and my entire being tinkled with the joy of having helped another human being. Later I was told that a gas canister had exploded while she was preparing food for her family. She had been severely burned and for a long period was very close to dieing. The younger of her two children had died in the accident and her husband had left out of despair. She had lost most of her mobility and as she was therefore incapable of taking care of her surviving daughter, who had fortunately been outside playing when the explosion took place, she had had to send the child to live with her sister far away.

That this gentle and unfortunate woman had the human generosity to show consideration for my discomfort in that situation is a fact I will never forget.

She taught me more about emotional intelligence and human compassion in a few minutes than any of the thick books I have read on the subject. It is not the act itself, but the motivation behind it that shows its real scope, and changes everything. She taught us that regardless of our economic resources or position in society, we all have the power to change the world for the better. Sometimes all it takes is a look of encouragement or a gentle squeeze of the hand to get the energy flowing.

On that trip I encountered the compassion, charity and tolerance that will forever be woven into my very soul. Because with many of these people, who literally had nothing, I experienced an inner calmness and a confidence in life that many of my wealthy business clients in the West could only dream of achieving. It was a profound and quiet faith in life, which amazes and inspires me even today.

We all have our own circle of influence in which we can have a positive effect on people around us. The question is not whether you alone can change the general course of the world, but rather what you can do right here right now within your own personal circle of influence – your sphere. It is not about tomorrow – it is about the now – and when you realize that you can in fact change the world, even if it is just a little bit, your own life changes for good.

Sebastian: When I heard you the first time in Denmark, somebody from the audience asked you what you would do if you were standing in the middle of a road and a mad dog came barking towards you. You answered him 'Get a stick'. Then, later the same afternoon, another person asked what you would do if it were a country that was aggressive. You sat for a long time, then you looked at the audience and said, 'Get a very big stick.' We all laughed, like we are doing now.

Then you explained that we look at any given action from different perspectives. On one hand the Chinese invasion meant pain and suffering to a lot of people but at the same time it opened the world for the introduction of Buddhism.

Dalai Lama: Leadership has to do with seeing things from a different perspective and at the same time staying true to your honest beliefs. If you stay true to the truth then you are on solid ground no matter what happens.

Ethics – our psychological backbone

'Man is not a species whose destiny lies within his congenital nature, but rather something you become through your actions and your realization.'
(Taken liberally from Georg Wilhelm Friedrich Hegel)

Ethics is commonly understood to be the perception of what is right and wrong in human behavior and mentality. As we grow up we are taught morals – the generally accepted standards of what is right or wrong in one's particular culture. They vary. Oscar Wilde believed morality to be 'simply the attitude we adopt towards people whom we personally dislike.'

The Danish poet, architect and artist Piet Hein said, 'The law of antipathy is simple: What you do not understand, you will dislike.' He stresses the need to focus on education and dialog if we wish to create a tolerant world.

We are born with strong inner ethics. And in my opinion our ethical foundation is a key element in the human psyche. Ethics is our psychological backbone. It is living and flexible, but if bent too far or too forcefully it will damage the overall functions of the entire organism.

If we go beyond our natural ethical boundaries our body and psyche will warn us to ease off. If the exertion continues, permanent damage can occur. Crossing your inherent ethical boundaries will give you long-term psychological problems, make you physically sick – and give you a permanent bad conscience. That is why it is so important – and extremely difficult – to get in touch with your core ethics…

We often meet people who have directly copied other people's way of life and actions without even reflecting on the ethical values that lay behind their behavior. At a later stage they have suddenly come to the realization that what they were doing was wrong – ethically.

Subsequently, many of them have a really hard time coming to terms with the consequences of their unethical behavior. Many wonder how they could have been so stupid as to be driven solely by their ego's vanity. Ambitious leaders and people in powerful job positions in particular can become so determined in their crusade for success that they sometimes neglect to listen to their inner ethical voice.

Finding your own ethical standpoint is often difficult because of strong influences and peer pressure from society and your surroundings. People often experience having to face the same ethical dilemmas over and over again. It is wise to take a break, analyze and search for the underlying cause of the problem. 'Life can only be understood backwards; but it must be lived forwards,' as Kierkegaard said, underlining the importance of being willing to learn. We all need negative experiences to strengthen our foundations, set our boundaries and make better ethical judgments.

Equality is an absolute core ethic

How unethical something is does not matter. It is your knowledge of it being unethical which should determine your actions. If something is unethical, it is unethical – it cannot be measured in degrees.

Kierkegaard's central message to us today is that we must consider our actions very carefully. In the Kierkegaardian world there are two juxtaposed opposites: necessity and possibility. Necessity signifies that which we cannot influence, e.g. the weather, and possibility means how we deal with the inevitable.

Kierkegaard maintained that every human being is unique,

and that every individual deserves to be treated equally no matter his or her status, leadership or position in society. Nobody understands this better than His Holiness the Dalai Lama, who treats everybody the same – beggars and presidents alike. It is an absolute ethical value that every human being is equally precious.

To be equal is not necessarily to be alike. And we are never completely alike, since every individual is unique. Equality is simply treating every person we meet with the same amount of respect, presence and dignity.

The boss and his employee have a different status in the workplace (the boss has the power to make the vital decisions, the employee does not). However, as human beings they are absolutely equal.

BUSINESS ETHICS

Most businesses exist solely to make as much profit as possible. Only a few innovative and socially aware businesses have recently started transgressing the emotional plane in their way of thinking. It is important to do it, but it is also important to stay true to the motivation for doing it. Sadly we see some companies branding themselves as socially responsible, though their only goal is to increase profits.

Today, multinationals have become so influential that they can alter many people's lives with a flick of a switch, without even having to concern themselves with the normal rules of democracy. Therefore Corporate Social Responsibility (CSR) has become a thing of utmost importance, and not just a fancy marketing gimmick.

But at least CSR, UN Global Compact standards and mega trends like 'Do-no-harm strategies' and 'Do-good strategies' bear witness that things are in motion. Finally.

Fortunately the consumers (you and I) are becoming increasingly aware of the ethical standards of business. A fact which has led to new ethically aware investment groups that only put money into environmentally aware, sustainable fair trade companies. Fair trade companies are currently enjoying huge success and showing other companies the way to consider more ethically sound alternatives.

Sebastian: What is pure business and what is unethical business?

Dalai Lama: It depends on the context – on where the business is conducted and the local standard of honesty. What is considered proper in one country may not be considered proper in another. The clarity of the perception of those doing the business is also important.

But the most important aspect in business is to be truthful. You should conduct your business honestly and in harmony with local ethical conventions. Then it is pure business.

Sebastian: So if it is relative, something considered pure business in one country could be considered unethical in another?

Dalai Lama: Yes, that would be possible – everything is relative – conventions and traditions are relative. Let me give you an example. Take the price of vegetables for instance. In the country where they are grown in large quantities, they are usually available at a very low price. In another country on the other side of the world those vegetables may cost 50 times as much. Why? Does that mean that some businessman is behaving unethically in making a huge profit? Not necessarily, because the packaging, the wages, the transportation, tolls and tax-

es, distribution and so on may add a lot to the price. So in order to distinguish between what is pure and what is unethical we need to know all the aspects of the particular business.

All things in life are relative – as is business. Prices will always vary from market to market, but you should never take advantage of people by charging more than is reasonable.

Sebastian: Surely some things are absolutely unethical? Child labor for instance?

Dalai Lama: Yes. Child labor should never exist in any part of the world, but it does. In India or Nepal for instance many poor families can only make ends meet if their children work too. Regrettably child labor has to be tolerated to a certain extent in some parts of the world for the time being. We have to stop it in all parts of the world, but it must be done over time.

You have to consider the practical aspects of ethical behavior. But ultimately all children everywhere should have a secure childhood with love, care and a good education – and not have to do hard labor.

Sebastian: So something unethical may have to be tolerated temporarily because of circumstances, but that will never make it ok?

Dalai Lama: Yes.

The next leap in evolution: Homo Spiritualis

*'The first sip from the grail of science
makes you atheistic – but on the bottom waits God.'
(Werner Heisenberg)*

In spite of almost identical DNA, every human being is uniquely distinct and one of a kind. It may seem paradoxical that we are so alike yet so distinct. Like snowflakes, we are all seemingly alike, yet uniquely different – there is only one copy of each of us.

And it is precisely in our unique core code that we find our connection with the divine. Inscribed in the basic human structure, in its very oscillating essence, lies a unique code ... a password to the divine – to God – to the inner nothingness.

You need not hook up via others. You have your own connection with God. We have reached the point in our evolution where we should all be able to connect to that for which there is no name.

The religions have played out their role as 'necessary mediums' between humankind and the divine – we now need to embrace our inherent divinity. It is encoded in every cell of our body – in every oscillation in our field of energy. Like an otherworldly treasure it is waiting to be explained.

We can learn from many different spiritual and religious traditions that every human being is extraordinary, remarkable and therefore essentially divine. Inside every human being there is a certain spark that some people call 'soul', some 'life' and some even 'the breath of God'.

Jesus, Mohammed and Buddha spent their lives narrating their personal stories to people, sharing their spiritual experience. They all believed that we are created in the image of God. Like the sea reflects the sun, God is reflected in humankind.

Our internal homing device

We all contribute to the eternal and divine light – it shines in us from the very beginning of our life. Like a homing device it directs us towards the divine – it leads us Home. There is a bond between man and divinity – the energy from whence everything originates.

The word religion originates from 'religare', which in Latin actually means 'to reconnect'. Through religion, we reconnect with every form of existence including all human kind. In Sanskrit language the word Dharma (Law) is used to denote this concept. This is the law binding everyone and everything together. In the Arabic language this law is known as Deen. In Chinese it is described as Tao.

Throughout their lives, people like Jesus, Mohammed and Buddha strived to help people reach a holistic level of consciousness. By mastering their own lives and liberating themselves from despair they conquered fear and became part of the eternal stream of life – a state which is possible for everyone to reach, if you have the will to do it.

God, eternity and all that

How can it be relevant to talk about God and eternity in a book about a sustainable future? The answer is as simple as it is important: Our cultural understanding of 'God' and eternity has significant influence on our daily behavior.

If you 'know' that you are here for one life only, you may very well opt for relatively short-term life strategies – because why start something that you cannot harvest yourself – and why change the way you live if you won't be facing the problems yourself? If, however, you 'know' that you are going to live several lives, this will naturally motivate most people to think and act with a more long-term vision. I remember working with a group of Japanese leaders several years ago. We spoke of five and ten-year plans for their companies when one of them reminded me of their 500-year vision. I had to think about that one for a bit and asked why they had SUCH a long-term vision. His answer was, 'Because then no one will be thinking of themselves only – no one will only think of what works in the short term – everybody will think about what is good as a whole – even after the individual has left – it offers better and lasting decision-making.' So our existential understanding does indeed determine our daily actions and therefore we must take into account the existential discussion of eternity when putting sustainability on the agenda. This does not mean that you cannot be a hard-core existentialist and at the same time be concerned with the environment and sustainability – this is very doable, of course.

For most people the connection between their existential starting point and how it influences their daily lives exists on such a deep and subtle plane that they may never become aware of it.

Our choices and approach to life are made with an often-unconscious understanding, through which all information is processed. And because this is the point of origin for all thought patterns, attitudes and actions, this is also where we must be mindful, investigative and self-correcting.

New wine in old bottles?

'In the beginning was the word', it says in Genesis. But maybe 'the word' is not to be taken literally as a sound, but figuratively as oscillation/energy. Like the Eastern word 'Om' that is said to be the first sound of the universe. Do these statements signify that A Creative Intelligence (God) started the Universe with an oscillation? Is God energy? Is this the answer everyone is looking for? The notion of God is indeed as slippery as a piece of wet soap.

In our time Quantum Physics has taken hold of the Universe, God and Eternity. Quantum physicist Fred Allan Wolf explains that the universe, which seems so tangible and rock solid, is in fact energy in flux – an oscillating field of energy. And since energy never ceases to exist, it must be eternal.

Science 'grants' us eternal life

I am convinced that some day science will be able to differentiate between the oscillations of the mind, body and spirit and help us to understand the incomprehensible. But already today we know that the sum of energy is constant. The physical law of energy maintains that all energy is constant. Matter transforms and takes another form but the sum of energy is constant. This means that energy is eternal and that is a difficult concept for most people to take in, because it seems as though everything in our physical world comes to an end at some stage.

But even though an abstraction like eternity can be hard to fathom for a human being with a fragile, ageing and tangible body, it is nevertheless a fact. When wood burns, matter is changed into heat/energy but nothing is lost. Energy is everywhere, in everything and in between. It has always been and will always be.

This fact stretches our mental capacity and makes us reach out to religion – especially when we relate its eternity to our own human existence. When we die the body disintegrates – but where does the energy go? I personally believe that because everything is energy and all energy is eternal, our soul energy is eternal. Essentially, that means that we too are eternal.

If this is ever proven, everyone with a classical Christian background will have something new to incorporate into his or her outlook on life and especially death.

Eternity can cause laziness

If everything is eternal is there any reason to act? To hurry? Buddhists who do nothing to influence the world in which we live, and Christians who believe that they live one life only, may need to reconsider things.

The concept of 'one life' calls for busyness (get it here and now!) and cynical behavior (don't let anybody get in your way). You must make the most of it while you are here. Over-consumption, unethical behavior and egotism automatically follow.

On the other hand, eternal lifecycles may give rise to docility since urgency loses its meaning. You may find yourself floating passively like driftwood on the ocean of life. Both are ways of avoiding responsibility.

Even though science has 'granted' us eternal life, it does not mean that we can just sit back and let things run their course. Our unity with the divine – the eternal energy – demands that we take responsibility.

A positively sustainable future for all humanity will only begin to realize itself when we truly understand that we are part of the universal energy – of life itself. We need to reach a harmonic state with eternity (through meditation) and fully manifest our individual divine power of creation.

We are slowly moving towards enlightenment. Recently I read that some space scientists believe that we have knowledge of only about 4% of the known universe, so a lot remains to be discovered. That goes for human life as well. We must continue to explore and never become stagnant in life or in our religious beliefs.

The Lotus flower

To balance challenge with skill is essential in all aspects of life for flow and progress. There is a Hindu metaphor for this meaningful relationship, which enables spiritual development: The lotus flower starts its progress by rooting itself in fertile mud (the physical plane). It then rises through the water (the emotional plane) to break through to the surface air (the mental plane). Finally, the flower opens up to the sun (the spiritual plane).

A beautiful description of the phases any human must go through to gain an insight into human existence. This metaphor can be applied to business as well, and when we do so it becomes crystal clear that there is still a long way to go. Most businesses are still only on the physical plane and that is why the business world needs special attention.

THE HUMBLE PROPHETS

Only a few people have ever reached their full human potential (homo spiritualis), but those who have, have had an enormous influence. Jesus, Mohammed and Buddha spent their lives telling others of enlightenment and the human potential.

They all believed that every single human being could transcend the earthly realm and thereby realize their highest human aspect. They each describe various ways of realizing your full human potential.

Other common factors were that they did not want to be worshipped, they never hoarded material goods, nor did they tyrannize people who had made other choices in life. They had found their own way of becoming enlightened. They were all humble, tolerant and self-sacrificial. Just imagine if all business leaders, politicians and judicial authorities were to abide by those basic principles.

No matter what tradition we have been brought up in, it seems obvious that coordination and cooperation – transgressing our outer physical differences – is the key to overcoming our common challenges and creating a sustainable positive future for everyone. A global collective endeavor that I am sure Mohammed, Jesus and Buddha want us to embark on together.

We already know

More and more people are questioning contemporary values, rigid traditions and our way of life. In my work as a business consultant for organizations worldwide, I have noticed that the majority of people feel very strongly that something is out of order. That the way we have set up our business systems – both locally and on an international scale – works perfectly when it comes to maximizing profit, but poorly when it comes to encouraging sound ethical behavior.

Maybe we all have an internal alarm founded in biological knowledge that goes off when something is wrong. Just as animals instinctively sense a landslide hours before it happens, and seek higher ground.

We simply know that things have to change. The insistent buzzer in the back of our minds demands it.

The existential question is as important for us spiritually as the law of gravity is physically. Sometimes the existential search for answers lies dormant until our basic needs are taken care of. But even when our basic needs are met it does not mean that everyone automatically starts searching for the meaning of life – far from it. Considering that most Westerners have already sorted their basic needs out, only an alarmingly small part of the population have actually awakened, and integrated ethical behavior into their everyday lives.

For many years now, many of us have been indulging in Western materialistic surplus without becoming the slightest bit happier. The reason for our lack of happiness, despite our materialistic wealth and plentiful consumption, is partly explained in Martin E. P. Seligman's The Psychology of Happiness, in which the author isolates three main forms of happiness: the physical, the mental and the profoundly meaningful. He shows, through a series of examinations of quality of life and feelings of happiness, that we cannot consume our way to happiness. He concludes that for human beings the feeling of being a part of – or taking part in – something, which is profoundly meaningful, endows us with immense strength and stamina.

The most common response to the fiercely imbalanced distribution of global wealth goes something like this: 'Well, it has been like that forever, and even though I would like to do something about it, there is nothing I can do personally …'

But all that is, is underestimating your own capabilities, and a way of placing the blame at somebody else's door. And the fact that it has been like that forever does not really justify anything, does it?

Sebastian: If everyone had reached the holistic state of consciousness would we even need leaders? (I know the Dalai Lama is really thinking hard about this one, because I have noticed that a certain happy expression comes across his face whenever he has to reach deep into his wisdom and contemplate complex matters.)

Dalai Lama: If everyone were on the highest level of consciousness – of holistic awareness – many things would be radically different. But there have always been those who were naturally better at leading and organizing than others, and that will probably always be the case.

In Buddhism we think in eons of time and believe that we should not attach ourselves to anything or anybody. Detachment from things that grab hold of your mind is the most important thing for everyone – especially for a leader. As I see it, many leaders have been caught by their own minds and are pinned down by their egos and yearning for power. I pray for them.

Making a difference

> 'Insanity is doing the same thing over and over
> – and expecting different results!'
> (Albert Einstein)

Time and time again, we hear the argument (which could also be called the excuse), 'But what can I do – one little person – to change these deeply ingrained causes?' My answer is always this, 'Do as much as you can with the resources that are available to you.' However little it may seem, your contribution is a step in the right direction.

You might feel that your government ought to do something about problems on a global scale. I suppose that expecting others to solve problems for you is one way of coping. Or maybe you simply find the problem too deeply rooted or too complex to handle. Perhaps you fear (perhaps rightly so) that trying to make a difference in the world is a course of action, which would take you way out of your comfort zone and possibly put you in harm's way.

Unfortunately many people choose to ignore what they know about the state of the world, rather than use their knowledge to change their ways. If knowledge does not change our behavior, it means we keep going down the wrong path – knowingly.

All around we see suffering, humiliation and desperation, and yet we keep going, hoping that some day someone will do something about it. Is it ingrained naivety? Or passive optimism? We repress the unpleasant feelings and thoughts with large intakes of medicine or other stimulants, or simply through mindless absorption of mass-produced, soul and brainless entertainment. In essence we are just running away from a reality too harsh to handle. Due to our need to take the edge off all the terrible things in the world, the entertainment industry has been booming for years. The selection of TV programs, computer games and movies is seemingly infinite – providing plenty of cheap thrills for everyone. But in spite of the powerful sedative generously made available by the entertainment industry, we still sense things are not right.

Radical innovation is needed

We have to stop making the same mistakes over and over again. There is no sense in making improvements on that, which is essentially beyond repair.

When it comes to the use and distribution of Earth's resources, we must rethink and take a new approach. It is not enough to talk about 'innovation'. I have faith in the scientists of the world, and expect a lot of help from them in redressing the balance and instigating positive development. But we cannot depend entirely on the men and women of science to hand us the cures for illness, for poverty and for over-consumption. What needs to be

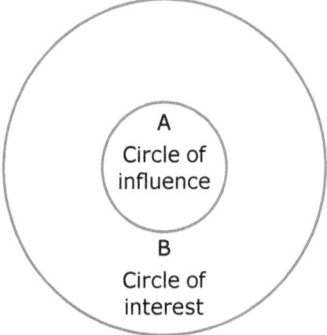

Figure: The spheres of influence

changed is too deeply ingrained for new research and innovation to reach it, and we need to take our action further than just treating the symptoms.

> **Ethical case**: A woman is home alone with her two young children – her husband is away on a business trip. One of the children is seriously ill and she is able to call the hospital and getting in direct contact with a doctor. In the evening the child grows increasingly sick, so she calls the hospital to speak with the doctor. The doctor would like to see the child, but since she is at home alone with not only the sick child, but also a newborn baby, she cannot leave the house and it will thus have to wait until the following day. The doctor says that if it is not too late when she finishes her night shift, she will stop by on her way home. Just after midnight, the doctor rings the doorbell.

The change must come soon, because the situation today is very similar to that of our forefathers 60,000 years ago in Africa. Once again, our species finds itself on a 'burning platform' threatened by extinction. Everything is starting to smell burned and singed. The biggest difference between then and now is that this time around we have brought it upon ourselves and that this time, we cannot emigrate from the problem.

It is hard to say, whether we have three, ten or 50 years in which to react, but one thing is for sure: it is urgent.
The cardinal key to success is for every human being to truly work his or her personal circle of influence, finding and acknowledging their own unique potential and learning to live in harmony with all fellow human beings. It means reevaluating on a larger scale, not only personal responsibility, but life itself, and thinking about why we are all here.

Sebastian: How can you transform peace and holistic awareness into an interesting topic for all people including businessmen and women, who have often been trained to be combative and competitive? How can you transform it from being just an old passive hippie thing to an active and prosperous endeavor?

Dalai Lama: Peace itself is not only a concern of the society or community. An individual needs peace in his or her life. Families need peace because a family that lives in peace with one another is a strong family.

A businessman or leader without inner peace also has a negative effect on his staff. His business won't work as well as it could. People in business must understand that there will never be peace if they are a mess internally. So to find peace and to help others find their inner peace is a relevant concern for all living beings.

From my point of view the concept of peace should not only be distributed with a passive approach. I don't think that peace just means not to disturb others. I think that peace in action brings happiness to others. An active act of peace is to bring individual rights to everyone in society because it will create the basis for a peaceful community.

It is sometimes interesting to look at a question from the opposite angle and if we do so with peace, I could ask if war has ever brought anything beneficial to society or has it meant nothing but destruction? I don't think that we can ever justify military action. Supposedly war should bring stability and prosperity, but it is a contradiction to think that peace can come out of war.

But I must admit that it's a difficult matter. Even if all wars stopped there would still be problems, disagreements and conflicts because people have different ideas of how to do things in life. And that goes for companies as well. We must learn to deal with these aspects even when we are fully involved and therefore tend to speak quite bluntly, and ultimately we must have peace as our common goal.

It is important for me to clarify that peace should not be a passive movement – peace in action is a very active thing.

Peace should be practiced in a very active way and not just be understood as something, which is passive. If you try to refrain from action, you become inactive and that has got nothing to do with peace – peace is a very active movement.

Courage to change what I can

'It is easier to kill a tiger with your bare hands than it is to still the mind.'
(Buddhist saying)

The past only serves as a foundation for a better future – but insight always manifests itself in the present.
In other words: there is no reason to deal with the past if it cannot serve to better the future – decisions are always made in the present. Yes, our human past is troublesome, to say the least, but to the extent that it serves as a foundation for a better common future, we must accept it and learn from it.

Based on our past we understand why the future is scary, but our insight calls for courage. Any human being can mobilize their inner strength, and transcend their individual inhibitions through courage.

The first step is to free yourself from your need for social acceptance. Freedom comes from within, and once you start making your own decisions, the surrounding inhibiting cultural values will no longer have any effect on you.

We must distinguish between a brave person and a coward. A coward is someone who appears calm on the outside; but if we look at a very brave person, that person is also calm on the inside.

This means that if you only look at the outside – which is a common mistake – and compare people, they look similar. But in reality, one could be a coward who, when facing tough challenges, immediately gives up. The other could be very brave and never give up, even faced with what is ten times as difficult as that of the coward.

Courage shines from the inside out, which is why we can remain calm.

One of the most powerful displays of inner liberation and courage the world has ever seen was when a single human being went up against the entire regime of China.

This man walked calmly out onto Tian'anmen Square – to stand in front of a moving military tank and block its passage with his body. In fact he was blocking the passage of the entire Chinese military parade. And he didn't budge. Even when the tank tried to go around him he kept putting himself right in front of it blocking its passage.

His act symbolizes the individual strength possessed by every human being. Having grown up with a ruthless oppressive regime, that man knew the consequences of his act of defiance. Yet he stood there – the individual vs. the system. I know that many consider him courageous, but perhaps he had just had enough. He had reached that point of no return where the only possible action is to react against your oppressors.

That man – standing there with his plastic bags – vividly proved to the world that a single ordinary person can change the world. In that moment he became an eternal symbol of freedom.

MEDITATION – A WAY TO FREEDOM

I have personally experienced how simple centering and calming of the mind and spirit can completely remove the overshadowing factors in our lives.

There are many ways to a peace of mind, but one that is constantly proving itself as one of the most effective, is meditation.

Through meditation we can come to an understanding of

who we really are. Our quality of life depends on whether we use our inherent ability to stay centered or not. The goal of meditation is to reach a holistic level of consciousness. To separate ego/personality from the soul/higher self.

Meditation calms the consciousness through focused awareness and develops inner quietness so you can hear your intuition. Meditation is the gateway to the spiritual realm.

Meditative practices are incorporated into most religions in some shape or form. We all have different names for it: praying, chanting, mantra, rites, but they all basically mean the same – to dissolve the ego into the collective consciousness of the universe ... God. Meditation enabled the founders of all religions to reach the holistic level of consciousness. They were the pioneers of meditation.

Many believe that Jesus got his extraordinary healing powers through the long-term practice of meditation; and the many places in the four gospels where Jesus 'retired to desolate places...' could also be interpreted as Jesus having a habit of meditating.

The Prophet Mohammed was in meditation before his revelations, and undoubtedly Moses did the same before receiving the foundation for Judaism from God on Mount Sinai. And it is hardly necessary to elaborate the important role of meditation in the Hindu, the Buddhist and the Jain religions. The problem is, however, that in Western society very few people are brought up knowing the full benefits of 'making the mind still'. Thankfully a great number of wise human beings have cleared the way for us. Through their practice, the benefits of meditation have become evident. The Dalai Lama gets up at 4 a.m. to meditate. Boutros Boutros-Ghali, the sixth Secretary General of the United Nations frequently used a meditation room in the UN building.

Celebrities, authors and artists such as Deepak Chopra, David Lynch, Brad Pitt, Madonna and Richard Gere have also done their bit to make meditation more mainstream – perhaps even trendy, in the good sense of the word.

As a result, meditation is much more accepted today, and is even being adopted in more and more businesses. I hold a lot of seminars where we teach exhausted and unhappy employees and leaders to relieve the stressful elements of work through meditation. And most people find it surprisingly easy to get started and learn the stress-relieving breathing techniques.

All you have to do – to tap into this enormous inner peace – is to push the reactivate button for a talent you already possess. Meditation is natural for both body and mind. It may take years to fully master the skill, but both you and the world around you will benefit from your having a calmer and clearer mind.

Although I cannot prove it scientifically, my many experiences with this phenomenon confirm my belief that meditation is a natural and inherent human quality. You can, however, prove scientifically that people who meditate can achieve a positive control over their minds, their emotions and even over certain body functions.

If you can change your own mental and emotional state, people around you will also benefit from it. This can be very handy if you find yourself in an emotionally hostile environment, where fear and greed are dominant, because you can learn to protect yourself from harm.

Daniel Golemann was one of the first to describe these inter-human relations in his book 'Destructive Emotions: A Scientific Dialogue with the Dalai Lama' where he shows that negative feelings in others result in physical discomfort for untrained receivers. But if the receiving party meditates on a regular basis, it is possible for them to train themselves to withstand or deflect the negativity of their surroundings. He argues that within certain Lamas the neural networks are 800% more developed than within people who do not practice meditation.

Research is turning up scientific proof that we are all interconnected. In the 1980's Giacomo Rizzolatti, Leonardo Fogassi and Vittorio Gallese discovered the mirror neurons in the brain. These are neurons that are not only activated when a person moves or experiences an emotion... but also when he or she observes the same movement or emotion in others.

The discovery was significant in the research of emotional relations; for instance how and why can we 'see' another person's mental state and feel empathy. In his book Why I Feel What You Feel Joachim Bauer explains how the mirror neurons in one person intuitively 'sense' how another person is feeling.

We are, in other words, built for empathy. Neurobiological resonance connects us all in a human collective network. We have empathy because we are herd animals. Empathy is a defining attribute of being human according to Preston and de Waal.

If you are not the prime minister of your country or a wealthy owner of a big company, but are still looking for an easy way to do something positive for the world (and for yourself), you can start by simply improving your own inner self through meditation. Whether you are a Muslim, Christian, Hindu, Jew, Buddhist or anything else, the only thing that matters is being Human.

Release your talent

For too many years we have focused entirely on 'effectiveness' and the left side of our brain. Now we need to catch up with and bring into play the many different forms of intelligence. Every human is naturally disposed to be able to master mental techniques that can guide us into finding deep inner peace, but, in most cases, we have never been properly encouraged or instructed in how to use these tools. I believe that deep in our biological system exists a lake so calm that not even the surrounding chaos of the world can cause the slightest ripple on its surface. It is waiting for us to dive in and become part of it.

As mentioned, many business people have begun to learn the techniques of meditation and with very positive results. Especially in connection with conflict resolution training. Because it is obviously a lot easier to solve conflicts when your inner core is in balance. Furthermore it becomes easier to deal with personal criticism (even harsh personal attacks) when you are able to focus on what is important.

By practicing simple meditation you can center your mind and avoid negative agitation. A negative conflict is classically characterized by emotionally charged communication, which manifests itself in various degrees of aggression.

When you meditate you become more emotionally stable and can avoid reacting negatively to unconstructive or unjust criticism. That will, more often than not, make it possible for you to diffuse the situation and resolve the conflict.

Many people who meditate also experience an improved ability to focus on what is important rather than on the immediate – a very useful skill for everyone, especially for a leader. So even though the origin of meditative tradition lies outside Western culture, we would be wise to adopt it. 'The mind is a good servant, but a lousy master', as the old saying goes.

OUR INTERNAL ETHICAL NAVIGATION SYSTEM

Through my work with various businesses over the years I have often seen that when people learn the skill of meditation, it helps them to dismiss their inner limitations and overshadowing. Therefore their internal ethical navigation system becomes free and boots up automatically and they begin to reflect their ethical core values in their decision-making.

It can be a tough and painful process to liberate your own mind – as Buddha himself could testify – but that should not stop you from pursuing it. It is fascinating and wonderful to observe the reawakening of the inner ethical navigation system in a human being, because it happens instantaneously and changes everything forever.

Intuition comes to our consciousness in two ways. In one way (the unconscious), intuitive insight strikes like lightning out of a clear sky and brings what could be described as epiphany.

The other way (the conscious) is to open the inner eye to reality as it is and not how we normally perceive it. The first way is overwhelming and beyond our control. We cannot count on it whenever we need it.

The second, however, is a method that can be taught and disciplined through meditation. It can fundamentally alter our perception and understanding of life.

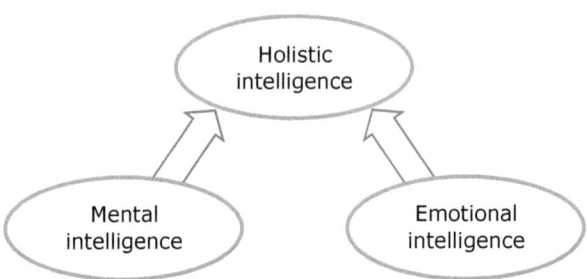

Intellect, emotions and intuition – the perfect triad

When working with intuition, it is never either/or, but a matter of balancing intuition with intellect. When instinct, emotions and mind work in harmony, it will secure a deep-rooted foundation for understanding reality.

Intuition brings spontaneity to our interpretation of a complex context. Intellectual powers then take over and analyze further, translate, verify and verbalize in logical terms that can then be communicated on.

Your mental development is all-important in enabling you to utilize your intuition in reality. The well-developed intellect processes intuitive experiences and makes them practically useful for us.

Western society and our educational system are clearly over-developed intellectually and under-developed with regard to intuition. Judgment can become so dominant that it automatically rejects spontaneous input – but when instinct and brain go hand in hand as a strong well-balanced unit, great art, groundbreaking science and new theological insights materialize.

How to release your intuition

According to the Italian psychologist Roberto Assagioli, development of your intuition can only occur when you reduce disturbance from other psychological functions. The churning noise of ever-present, yet fleeting thoughts often keeps your consciousness occupied and blocks out the intuitive channels, because they distract your inner attention field – and we are drained of energy. The main factors that preoccupy your mind or block your intuitive channels are:

- A dominant intellect that cannot open up to new and different impressions
- An intellect that cannot interpret, formulate and comprehend the abstract, due to lack of education and training
- Big feelings that swell up and make it impossible to examine the idea neutrally.

A healthy and sound mind in a sound body is the key to your intuition, and this is where meditation comes in. Through meditation you can learn to still the mind to the point where you will hear the sound of your inner ethical navigation system.

The intuitive sense of what is right and what is not will, when it is fully operational, serve as your guide to your own divinity – to truth.

And when you combine your intuition navigation system with your 'homing' devices you will be a genuine Homo Spiritualis.

What is the cure?

Dr. C. Otto Scharmer and his team from the Massachusetts Institute of Technology (MIT) have developed a theory of change and renewal called Theory U.

His notions of 'letting go' of the dated patterns and convictions of the past in order to gain from the future and 'letting come', agree with the already recognized principles of setting yourself free from the past in order to shape the future – and change it for the better. If we understand everything through concepts of the past, we cannot move beyond it.

In our Western industrial society, effectiveness was always an indisputable positive value. Whether or not we have surpassed a knowledge-based society still remains to be studied, but Earth has become flat once again and the global village a reality.

We must acknowledge that a sustainable future is a global phenomenon and not just a national endeavor – and that calls for new concepts.

We are the sum of our actions

As conscious beings we can no longer afford to overlook the negative effects our irresponsible behavior has on the world around us and on our fellow kind.

We must take responsibility and act against non-ethical behavior. We must tap into our basic genetically programmed human sense of what is right and what is wrong and set it in motion. We must navigate from our core ethics – not our moral code, which is a relative and cultural phenomenon.

Our animal fear of being separated from the herd can sometimes sway us from doing the right thing. The fear of being left out is a force to be reckoned with, and will sometimes cause us to turn a blind eye to injustice.

Sebastian: What kind of economic system contributes the most in creating value for humanity?

Dalai Lama: When I was in China, we often heard about the negative sides and the dangers of capitalism. But now I think that a combination of the best values from socialism and the advantages from capitalism woven together would be most beneficial.

The form of capitalism we see in the world today is too combative in its nature. And if the entire economic system is based solely on capitalism, it is bad. It is a rather difficult matter to give a short answer to, because the economic system is interrelated with the political system and the world situation in general. So to say that capitalism is bad is to simplify things too much.

We have to look at the economic system as part of a larger structure, like a part of the body. You cannot judge the total state of the body just by observing that the lung is in excellent shape. The lung interrelates with the other organs. Everything is interdependent.

When we look at socialism we see that it was meant to support and benefit a large group of people, but the reality was different. Without democracy, freedom of speech and independent labor movements, the population suffers much more than they would within a capitalistic system with democracy, with equal laws, free speech and a free press. So we can't judge, just by picking on the economic system without consideration of all the other factors and situations.

But if a capitalist thinks only about profit and never considers how to distribute the surplus to everyone, then he or she is unbalanced – and greed will set in.

From a Buddhist approach we speak of balanced individualism – and we have a holistic outlook on the world, and that way of thinking will be really important for our common future.

Sebastian: So to take the best of both systems and weave it together with a holistic long-term vision would create a more sustainable future?

Dalai Lama nods.

Wisdom in action

*'God give me a peace of mind to accept the things
I cannot change, the courage to change the things
that I can, and the wisdom to see the difference.'*
(Marcus Antonius or Mark Antony)

Below is the essence of the wisdom of numerous teachings around the world. When actively applied to everyday life, these four principles can ensure a sustainable future – because they will set our inner wisdom in motion.

THE FOUR PRINCIPLES FOR A SUSTAINABLE FUTURE

Vision	To be able to dream – the utopian dream of community
Courage	To defend human ethics – even when faced by a superior power
Ability to change	To let go of the negative patterns of the past – and act freely
Ethical behavior	To know we are One People – and act accordingly

GIVE AND BE BLESSED

When you have more resources than you need to secure your own foreseeable future, you should channel the rest to those in need. Then you are truly blessed.

What would happen if every person and every wealthy company in the world decided to give away 10% of their own capital reserves and of all future profits – and redistribute it to sustainable development projects? Well, the world would suddenly be a new place. The entire world as we know it would change. It would give the human race a truly new and solid foundation for global trust, peace and creativity. A large number of conflicts all over the world would cease to be. And given enough time, the huge spending on the military would decrease and eventually that could be redistributed into sustainable development as well.

This utopia may seem far off – and far out for some people – in the light of the current global situation, but each person's sincere hope helps make the seemingly improbable a little less so. One day, it will happen. History has shown us that sometimes it only takes a few brave human beings to break the patterns and change the course of the world.

Non-violence

Non-violence is a very strong element in our common ethical code. Almost everyone is against violence – at least in principle. There is one tradition and one person in particular who knows how to translate ethical principles into practical action. Thanks to the Dalai Lama's never-ending patience and continued effort to have the Tibetans remain non-violent, the international community has finally discovered Buddhism.

For some, it is difficult to understand how non-violence can be a choice based on conviction, and they tend to interpret it as a weakness. Others understand the purpose and the concept of non-violence, but have a hard time dealing with their own personal fears and actually living out its principles.

As the philosophical (and religious) leader for the Tibetan people, His Holiness the Dalai Lama and his people have suffered severe humiliation and cruel oppression, but never once compromised the principle of non-violence.

In the early days of the hostile Chinese takeover and unjust occupation of Tibet many were dubious about the non-violent strategy. Some observers concluded that the Tibetan's passive resistance policy was simply due to China's superior force, but history has proven such conclusions wrong, and people's puzzlement with the Tibetans has turned to admiration and they have become an inspiration for many.

The Dalai Lama has said that even though the Chinese occupation has had incredible costs for the Lama personally, and the people, it has in no way influenced his commitment to non-violence. In 1989 this won him the Nobel Peace Prize and inspired people all over the world to rethink their lives.

It commands respect to listen to Tibetans who have undergone severe torture say that their biggest fear was of losing their ability to feel compassion for their torturers...

Do not kill ...

Do not kill
Do not kill the person next to you ...
Do not kill his dreams, his hopes – or his sprit.
Do not kill Do not kill him fast by shooting him
Do not kill him slowly by letting him starve
Do not kill him with degradation
Do not kill him out of fear
Do not kill him by forcing him to repeat your mistakes
Do not kill him by 'out-smarting' him in business
Do not kill him with your superiority
Do not kill him out of frustration
Do not kill him because he has a different culture or religion
Do not kill because if you do, you kill what's human in you
Do not kill

Tibetan wisdom has spread all over the world and has helped many Westerners, myself included, to reflect on life and its meaning – particularly due to the extensive travels of His Holiness the Dalai Lama around the world.

His shining Buddhist wisdom evaporates all misty shadows. Global human development would benefit tremendously if modern business integrated elements of Buddhist wisdom such as compassion, karma and humility. And if it were brave enough to live according to its principles.

In the following, I have summarized everything I have learned from religion, philosophy, common sense, work – and life in general – in the human ethical code:

The Code for Ethical Humans

- I am sincere in everything I do
- I carry my part of our collective responsibility for the Earth, other human beings and all life
- I know that love is the highest order and acknowledge my non-violent nature
- I utilize my full inherent potential and my entire circle of influence every day
- I give authentic feedback and object to any injustice I encounter
- I act responsibly and respectfully; I do things in a sustainable manner
- I do not engage in activity, which can be harmful to myself, others or the environment
- I believe in life and help all the people I encounter to unfold their true potential
- I know that everyone has a right to equality and a right to be different
- I know that everyone is an important part of humanity's eternal existence
- I know that I am part of one unity – one Earth, one people – and act accordingly in all my decisions.

Dalai Lama: I remember when a rich Indian family from Bombay came to see me here. They asked for my blessing and I told them, 'You are a wealthy family – that is also a blessing'.

I think that to make your own personal wealth grow, you need profit, but as we said before, 'you should make sure to contribute to your local community by financing for instance education, other training and facilities to help those not as fortunate as yourself. That's the way to get a good blessing,' I told them.

When we then look at this from a global level, like, for instance, in some of the nations in Africa, things become more complex. In some of these countries everybody is so poor that they need help from other countries. Still I find it very important that they themselves work hard to improve their lives. They should not be content with their ancient way of life, but should be supported by the richer part of the globe with education, training programs and equipment so the people, eventually, can secure their own future. It is important that they do the work themselves.

The rich side has so much confidence, vision and determination. And that is very important to have I always tell people.

So to be met with negativity just because you are rich is not right. In India for instance, the so-called untouchables – the lowest-caste Hindu group – sometimes have very negative feelings towards the higher castes, which won't help solve the problem. It will only lead to more hatred and violence, which evidently creates more distance. So, from my point of view, the first step of the way for them is to study well, work hard, be honest and have self-confidence, but at the same time the rich side must provide them with training materials, education and trust. This is my view.

Sebastian: Through my aid work in the Tibetan society I have seen people who are granted a personal sponsorship without any demands and see it as an opportunity to change their lives. They quickly take charge and start an education or a small business. But for others, aid can create a very passive orientation that sometimes leads to a de-motivation to work at all. Because it is easier to just receive the money. It's a problem that all aid organizations must be aware of.

Dalai Lama: It is very true. The aid spoils some people.

Sebastian: So it is important that aid programs always make the receiver as active and self-sufficient as possible. Many of the NGO programs provide help in making a business strategy and give soft loans, without interest to get people started.

Dalai Lama: That is very good. If you have one without the other, it is no good. If people have initiative without money they cannot do anything. Likewise if people have money without any direction it is no good either. I think, like you do, that soft loans combined with guidance, is the proper way to help. If you just give some money you cannot be sure that it will be put to the best of use. I heard that after the Tsunami disaster, some of the donations they received were misused because they didn't know how to spend them wisely. In some cases to get a lot of money without knowing how to put it to good use, I heard, could turn people into alcoholics or drug addicts, which is very dangerous.

Sebastian: In other words the financially richer sides should help the poor sides by strengthening them and their countries from the inside through education of all the people, sharing of knowledge and ethical investments and soft loans. And never should we keep them prisoners by just giving them enough to keep them passive.

Dalai Lama: Yes. The rich side must provide education, schools and the required knowledge to use the material facilities they donate.

Right from the beginning I have always stressed that we Tibetans must build our community in India as if we were going to remain here for a hundred years. When the situation changes, it is very easy to go back, but it has to be when the time for a proper return is right. When that happens, we can easily go back to Tibet and we may offer what we have here to the Indian community.

Some Tibetans might want to stay and become Buddhists in an Indian territory. I remember that right from the beginning we have had this discussion in the Tibetan society. In the early 1960's we sent Tibetans to South India to create settlements. Many Tibetans, including my older brother, were very much against that decision. Some Tibetans felt that that was too far away and that it could possibly be harmful for the Tibetan spirit. They said that it was so far away from Tibet that they felt that they could never go back. But the Tibetans in the South India want to return to Tibet just as much as any other Tibetan anywhere.

Therefore, if you are well established here in India or Nepal, both economically and business-wise, you are in a better situation and have a choice, when the changes come. If you remain poor, then there is no choice, and that is very difficult. If the economy is poor because there is too little business, then it is very hard to preserve the Tibetan culture.

Mere enthusiasm will not do it.

But if we have sufficient money and resources, we can preserve Tibetan identity and culture ourselves – and with dignity. It doesn't matter how much enthusiasm you have because enthusiasm doesn't do it alone.

Change through work and business

> 'We cannot solve our problems with the same
> thinking we used when we created them.'
> (Albert Einstein)

If you have been mentally programmed early on in life to perceive work in a certain manner, you are prone to stick to that perception throughout your life.

In many places in the world it is common to inherit your father or mother's profession. You may not be disposed for that sort of work and you may not want to do it. But most likely you will end up doing it, unless you really make an effort to pursue your own personal potential.

In most areas of the world leadership automatically grants you high social status as a citizen and is therefore highly sought after by everyone, including those who may not be disposed to being good leaders at all.

This strong work-related programming in most human beings causes incredible problems in the business market and can be explained through our relentless striving for profit. It is therefore necessary to examine the dynamics of today's employment and business life in greater detail.

Changing our approach to our working life is a good place to start, since the activity known as 'work' takes up an enormous amount of our life both mentally and physically.

Many of the existentialistic dilemmas we experience in our daily lives occur in a work environment. When we put together human consciousness, mental dynamics and work/business we enter a new dimension, where it seems that the negative traits of human nature aggressively accelerate.

That is why work and business is exactly the area where we need to change things around, and why my interviews with The Dalai Lama focus on working life and business.

To own, to lead and to be led

Our approach to work and business can take on three forms:

- We can own
- We can lead, and
- We can be led

Pure business

The term 'pure business' denotes a business, which is ethically sound and positively sustainable on all accounts.

Let us then dive straight into the discussion of what is ethical and sustainable – i.e. 'pure' – in a business context. We have all encountered the unethical: e.g. products containing harmful ingredients, deceitful salespeople, corrupt government officials, etc.

Unethical is when you act in spite of your knowledge to the contrary. If we do not know any better, our actions can be devastating, but they can hardly be called unethical. But when we do know better, we must act accordingly and change our actions.

Does the tobacco industry know that their product causes harm to the health of their customers? Do candy companies know that the coloring agents and the food preservatives they add to their products can cause harm to their consumers – especially if they are young? Do people in the medical industry know they produce medicine and drugs that are actually not designed to cure, but only to stabilize the disease, so as to ensure the medical company lengthy and stable revenue? When they test new products on third world populations – do they know that they are experimenting with human life?

To protect the rights of the consumers many societies have set up control systems, which try to keep the business industry and its products in check. But essentially we know that it is virtually impossible to monitor everything; and is it not ethically unacceptable that we have to?

We must strive for a level of holistic consciousness where nobody would even consider selling rotten meat, or producing medicine that deliberately only stabilizes the disease, or medicine which has side effects that are far worse than the sickness itself.

WHY CHANGE THE WORLD THROUGH BUSINESS?

You are selling a bad product when you know it contains destructive agents for the consumer. It is simply unethical – impure business – to sell products like tobacco, guns and drugs. But what about processed food products that have highly refined or added, 'invisible' sugar or fat in large amounts? Many nutrition experts argue that these foods too are bad for the body.

However, for the businesses whose entire production and revenue is based on these refined commodities, it can be very difficult to acknowledge and integrate this new nutritional research. For them it is much easier to overlook and refute the new knowledge.

Often there are enormous economic interests at play and the balance of power is not easily shifted. Many of the food industry's big sub-industries have an annual turnover of hundreds of billions of dollars, similar to the candy industry; and with such immense economies it is easy to see why it can be difficult to admit that your empire is built on an ethically shaky foundation. It is common knowledge that for decades companies and corporations have been paying scientists huge amounts to 'contaminate' research results and counter new information that could harm the companies' interests.

The most famous – or infamous – case of scientific corporate misinformation was unraveled when the tobacco industry was forced to release internal reports. The reports showed beyond any doubt how unethical their business conduct had been and how harmful their product was to their consumers – the smokers. According to the Wall Street Journal, it was the longest-running campaign of misinformation ever to have taken place in the history of modern business – a bit of an achievement when you think about it.

Currently it is the effect of global warming that, until recently, was undergoing such a campaign – a corporate reaction against the obvious environmental symptoms. James Hansen from NASA said, 'The goal is not to win the debate, but to keep it going. Because when people hear the scientists disagree, their reaction is to say, "Come back when you have settled the argument."'

And so you pacify the consumers who continue their mindless spending and happy over-consumption – which of course brings in money to the global industries that keep wrecking our lives.

> **Ethical case**: A saleswoman attended a kick-off meeting prior to the launch of a new medical product and all participants were excited about the product's many advantages for the consumer (people with life-threatening diseases). The saleswoman asked why it was triple the price of previous products, as she would like to have her arguments ready before being asked herself. The answer was: 'It didn't have to cost more than the old product – but they (the consumers) are going to go crazy over it, so they will be willing to pay whatever we ask.' She stood up, looked straight at her own sales manager, quit and left.

But just because we are up against great forces and economic powers does not mean that we shouldn't react. We must not refuse to acknowledge the facts, and just let things lie for as long as we did in the case of the tobacco industry hoax.

Even today it is still legal in some parts of the world to sell deadly products – tobacco – with no restrictions at all. We cannot afford to have such a long reaction time – because this time the Earth's ecosystem and our entire existence as a species are on the line.

In time, everyone will become aware that refined food products filled with preservatives are not healthy for human beings. And in time even those responsible for the horrible fact that most medical companies often limit their research to stabilizing an illness, rather than curing it, will realize that what they are doing is highly unethical.

'You must be very scared'

Some human beings, however, are so overcome by fear, greed or egocentric ambition that they are willing to benefit from the suffering of others. These people, both in business and medicine, must be playing see no evil, hear no evil to be able to overlook the symptoms in the world and repress the incessant chime of their inner ethical alarm clock – which must be going off like crazy, having been put on snooze over and over again.

Deep inside they know that what they are doing is unethical and treacherous to themselves, to the entire humanity. Think of Gandhi looking at the soldiers pointing their guns at him when they came to arrest him and saying, 'You must be very scared'. Let us hope that these people will wake up soon. If you own a business that produces unethical goods, you must rethink the company's entire commercial basis, and start undergoing the necessary process of change and modification to regain your ethical bearing as quickly as possible.

If you are an employee or a middle leader of an unethically

based company, it is your personal responsibility to make your influence count in all possible matters and actively push your superiors or the owners to make the necessary changes. If you are unsuccessful in swaying the opinions of the people in charge, you must deal with the consequences and possibly resign. It sounds very simple ... and, in a sense, it is. It is all about courage, momentum and critical mass. If the majority of workers, employees and leaders say no to unethical work and production, then the businesses will have to change their method of production. Indeed, many people make excuses when it comes to their own personal responsibility: food, clothes, children's education, rent, mortgage, etc. – but if we continue to let ourselves be tied down by the material things, we can never progress to truly follow our human ethical core.

Even if you are employed by a company that only indirectly helps sell unethical products, e.g. a marketing company, you should still make your opinion count. There are many ways to go about it, but essentially, if you cannot convince your company to stop marketing clients who sell unethical products, you should resign.

In principle you should take action and quit, even if your employer only has one unethical client out of 50 pure businesses. Your action counts. If we keep accepting what we know is wrong without reacting against it, we are in fact justifying unethical behavior.

It's about our survival

The fact is that the all-consuming (economic) growth paradigm we keep imposing on ourselves, is indeed threatening our entire physical survival and existence.

Each year the Earth produces a huge amount of resources – more than enough for everybody. Yet frighteningly, if the 50 largest corporations in the world actually met their goals of 11-15% annual growth, there would be nothing left. We must re-evaluate these egotistic and insane goals.

As the Cree Indian saying goes, 'Not until the last fish has been caught, the last river poisoned and the last tree cut down, will the white man realize that you cannot eat money.' This tough ethical approach may sound harsh, and sometimes it is much easier said than done. It is nevertheless the right thing to do. In my interview with the Dalai Lama we touched upon a second possibility where – instead of 'just' leaving your job and having another person fill your place – you try to change things from the inside out. As you will see, this approach can be very constructive, but it takes courage and strong integrity, humility and a willingness to sacrifice.

There is nothing wrong with economic wealth in itself – it is how we acquire it and how we spend it that has caused global economic imbalance. The result is that an elite few have enormous reserves, while others are literally starving to death, and that simply makes no sense at all from a holistic perspective.

The musician and activist Bono said, 'Africa is not a cry for help. It is a catastrophe', but more and more regions on Earth are falling behind, and those who could – and should – take action, hold their tongues or dare not speak. Their silent acceptance is a treacherous act against all mankind.

Complexity poses new demands

In the current global business environment it no longer suffices to produce the best product.

You must exist as the best brand in the consumers' awareness and you must make your product readily available all over the globe.

Running a business is becoming increasingly more complex: branding, meeting/predicting the demands of your consumers, having the right values, keeping costs down, orienting yourself globally, making your company an attractive place to work, in order to get the best employees; and on top of all that you must run your business ethically.

It is easy to see how some businesses find it very difficult to meet all these demands.

Most business owners and top leaders who have responsibility for the overall business decisions are well aware of what is genuinely the right thing to do, but like so many, they are completely stuck in the old capitalistic maximum growth paradigm and cannot act freely; including when it contradicts their ethical core values

Furthermore, man is a social animal who seeks social acceptance – and aspires to status in society. Positive aspiration is one thing, but, as we have seen historically, egos tend to swell when they reach the very top of the social hierarchy. So, on all accounts we must change the hierarchal traditions of the past in an effort to cope with the complexity of current life.

CHANGE FROM THE INSIDE OUT

If a company reacts out of fear of bad publicity, it is just another motivation to avoid change. If we are hoping for the change to be permanent, it must come from the inside out. Management and employees must know that they cannot possibly continue manufacturing a product that causes harm to the consumers.

It can indeed be a costly affair to reevaluate and change your production. You might have to discontinue ethically unsound products that are earning you good revenue. Accept it. See it as a natural step of your business' evolution and try to make the loss of revenue temporary. It must be done.

Loss of revenue is no excuse to continue unethical business behavior.

Ethical case: A new truck driver needs to transport a truck full of pigs for slaughter in another country. He meets with his boss to go over the route. When he gets home, he starts to doubt, whether it is allowed to keep the animals enclosed for that long. He remembers watching a show about it once on TV, but he is unsure of the regulations – so he googles them. It turns out that the route his boss gave him is too long. The following morning – when he is supposed to leave – he has a meeting with his boss and shows him the printout of the regulations. His boss offers him 200 bucks to stop his silliness and get going. He says no thank you and that he would like to do the trip, but that it must be altered so that it is legally responsible. His boss gets very angry and says that he has 'no damn right to doubt him'. The driver leaves and, after consulting his union, reports his former boss to the police.

GUIDELINES FOR ETHICAL BUSINESS OWNERS:

- An ethical business owner only produces sustainable products and services
- An ethical business owner encounters everyone with dignity
- An ethical business owner is fair, truthful and ethically responsible in all matters
- An ethical business owner of a successful company always finds ways to support the less fortunate
- An ethical business owner invests in sustainable profit
- An ethical business owner makes his or her influence count to the benefit of the community
- An ethical business owner knows that he or she is a part of the entity – one globe, one people – and acts accordingly in all his or her business decisions.

The myth of 'Only the strong survive'

Many people say that they have two different sets of rules: one for work and one for their personal life. I have met people who readily admit that they leave their human capacity for empathy behind when going to work.

Where do they leave it? In a Tupperware container in the fridge at home? In the car in the parking lot? Or do they bottle it? What happens if they forget to bring it out after work?

Maybe, if it is left there long enough, it will dry out and shrivel up into a little hard raisin that will make a funny rattling noise when you shake the container? Seriously, you cannot leave your human consciousness behind like that. You cannot turn it on and off like a light switch.

If challenging such statements by suggesting that a person is the same human being independently of his or her geographical or organizational position, you are often met with the argument that if you cannot separate your work life from your personal life, you will not survive for long in 'real corporate life'.

'There is no room for compassion'; 'only the strong survive'; 'if you can't handle it, somebody else will', the arguments go.

Something about these statements seems wrong. Statements like 'don't take it personally, it's only business' and 'cynicism goes with professionalism'; take me back to the savanna 60,000 years ago and our prehistoric ancestors. To a time when we were primitive hunters surviving on nature by using physical skills.

Have we not evolved beyond that? Well, apart for the suit and the cell phone, the basic behavior seems unchanged. We need improvement and refinement of our ethical apparatus to prevail over our need to hoard goods and profit.

Profit, in itself, makes no sense – making money through sustainable production does. Pure business means to produce, sell and provide service in a sustainable, dignified and beneficial manner for everyone.

Sebastian: Is it good for human beings to work?

Dalai Lama: It depends on the quality of the work, but in general it is good to use your capacities.

Sebastian: Say you work for a company that manufactures plastic toys and you notice that a lot of waste is being thrown into the river. Suppose you have to support three children – do you say anything about the waste, or is the fear of losing your job going to stop you?

Dalai Lama: This is again a relative question. You need to provide for your family as well as being ethical. Do as much as you can to change the method of production. If you are in no position to decide that the company should stop this pollution, then you have to look at your abilities and other possibilities of employment. If you cannot find another job, then care as much as you can for nature in your spare time.

Sebastian: If you work in a facility that manufactures cloth and it often makes you so dizzy that you walk into things, but your manager says that if you are not able to manage the job, there are many others who can. What do you do then?

Dalai Lama: If you get sick from your work, you need to look for another job. Your health is more important than your job.

    I realize that the consequences of being without a job, without income, can be devastating – and if one person rejects a job, another person will happily take it – but the unethical behavior must stop. It requires individual courage.

True leadership

*'It is not because things are difficult that we dare
not attempt them. It is because we do not dare
that things are difficult.'*
(Seneca)

Human beings have a long tradition of hierarchical structures in societies and cultures where a few fortunate ones at the top of the pyramid have all the power, wealth and opportunity. At the bottom are the weak and the poor. This model goes back to our animal roots when the group or the herd was always led by an alpha individual, male or female, who was the undisputed top of the hierarchy. One could claim that it is natural for us to arrange it that way – and yes – it would be, if it weren't for the mere fact that we have evolved – so to me, it is reminiscent of the primitiveness of the past. We are SO much more than gregarious animals and that is what we need to put to use.

The model must somehow be rooted deep inside human experience since we are finding it so incredibly difficult to move beyond it. Seen in a modern business context, and in the light of the next evolutionary step for the human race, the hierarchy has to go. As the world we inhabit is becoming increasingly complex, we are each becoming more specialized professionally.

That is why there is a need for a new and more dynamic form of leadership/ decision-making process. It is called 'actualized leadership' and will eventually replace traditional hierarchical leadership. The essential principle of actualized leadership is that each individual naturally assumes leadership for the entire group when the topic/ challenge is something in which he or she is an expert, and thus ensures the best possible foundation for making the right decision for the entire group. This is a topic I deal with in my other book Inner Leadership and, to give you a brief description, it consists in the fact that you, as a leader at your workplace, possess power. There is nothing wrong with having power in itself. It is only when the power is used unethically that it becomes harmful. The more powerful your position at work, the more necessary it becomes for you to have a strong and sound ethical foundation.

Inspiration

A key part of good leadership is being able to inspire your employees. But what does it mean to inspire another human being and is it always a good thing? I mean, you could also say that Hitler 'inspired' people.

The etymology of the word is 'in' and 'spirit'. In other words, we awaken the spirit – the spiritual power – in the person we inspire, and when inspiration is strong, a person's spirit will become vibrant and empower him or her to overcome all challenges.

If our spirit supports our actions, everything we do becomes meaningful, and this is the strongest motivation possible. How many people around you are divinely inspired in their job and find happiness, 'in spirit' and deep meaningfulness in their work?

Most people see their job as something they need to do in order to make money. But it does not have to be that way. It is important to have a job that satisfies you – something that is meaningful; just think about how many hours of your life you spend working.

> **Ethical case**: A woman works in the subscription department at a newspaper. One morning and old lady calls because her newspaper was not delivered. She says that she really misses it as she cannot go out because she can no longer walk very well. It is so late when the old lady calls that there is not enough time to order a new newspaper to be delivered. The employee in the subscription department looks at the address and realizes that it would not be much of a detour for her to bring it by on her way home from work. So, a few hours later, she brings a copy of that day's newspaper by the old lady's house.

Could inspiration mean simply to spark the intense force of life inherent in every human being? To vitalize the life energy of that person? An inspirer should never inspire for personal gain, but to help someone realize their potential or for the joy of seeing the inspired person blossom. A leader who understands that is the best leader possible.

There are indeed leaders like that. The attentive leader, who makes room, shows faith and willingly engages in dialog, is a leader who will experience the joy and receive the reward of seeing the full personal and professional potential of the employee.

Work is an essential part of adult life and as psychologists Jean Lave and Etienne Wenger show so clearly in their book, Situated Learning, a balance between skill and challenge is vital for success, progress, joy and learning.

THE OLD LION

We have all met people in positions of leadership who display a primitive way of thinking, and have seen how that leads to negative actions. I remember a leader who was very much against

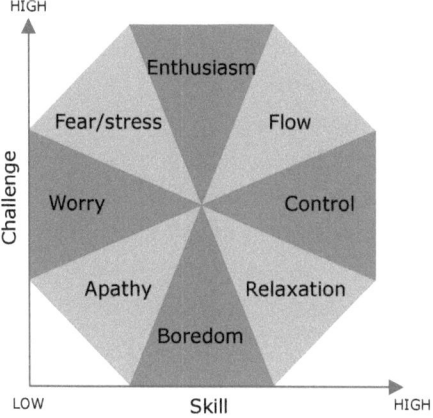

The perfect balance between Challenge and Skill (Mihaly Csikszentmihalyi, Flow)

change. He told me straight out that he was not interested in such 'fancy organizational mumbo jumbo'. I watched him pace back and forth in his office. Clearly, this was a man who suffered from very low self-esteem, and who feared being labeled incompetent. He had cleverly hidden his fear behind a veil of power and brutality.

He reminded me of a TV documentary I had recently seen about lions, in which the old male lion when defeated by a younger male must watch his offspring being killed by the victorious male. In the wild the newcomer is simply making sure that his own offspring will have the best chance of survival – but in this case it served as a precise metaphor for what was going on business-wise.

This primitive form of leadership, known as 'strong man' leadership, is also seen in politics – when you have a representative person (or a group) who is not afraid to make brutal decisions.

I am happy to say that the 'strong man' era is coming to an end, as the world is becoming increasingly complex, and as nobody can accomplish everything on their own.

The challenges we face demand a collective sharing of leadership, rather than the out-of-date hierarchical structure with a patriarchal oracle at the very top.

As a leader in the workplace, you have power. Having power is in itself not a bad thing. Only when power is used unethically does it become harmful. The more powerful position you have in the workplace, the more you need to have a strong and sound ethical foundation.

True leadership consists of ethical strength, empathy and a holistic vision.

> **Ethical case**: En employee is summoned to the leaders who ask him to keep an eye on a new employee, who was just transferred to their department because, as the leader says, 'I need an excuse to fire him – because I just don't want someone like him in my group'. When the employee declines to spy for the leader, the leader threatens to put him on the list as well. The employee gets up, goes directly to the top leader and tells about it – but ends up being fired himself – due to disloyalty. But he has no regrets.

Guideline for those who lead others:

- A leader understands his or her own potential
- A leader is humble and includes others in the decision-making
- A leader is truthful
- A leader knows that everyone is equal and respects the choice of others
- A leader accepts that he or she cannot always be popular with everyone
- A leader prioritizes sustainability over profit

Honest work

'It is honest work', we say ... but what exactly does it mean? For many people, their job is something they do because they have to. It is a joyless obligation. Something you do simply to earn money. A survey carried out by Gallup among nearly two hundred thousand people showed that 80% found that their job did not let them fully use all their talent – their entire human potential.

On a beach in India a group of people are cutting a ship up for scrap. They work hard with no safety equipment despite the extremely dangerous nature of the work. The economic reward they will receive for their endeavors is minimal. If they had other opportunities to make a living, they would probably take them.

In other places in the world miners work deep in dangerous mines where virtually no safety measures apply. The safety for the workers has been sacrificed to maximize profit for the owners. Both workers and owners know it.

On turkey farms across the world the workers feed the birds tranquilizing nerve medicine – if they did not, these territorial animals would peck each other to death.

In retirement homes everywhere, the everyday routines and schedules for the care workers are so tight that there is no time for holding a lonely old person's hand – at times not even when the person is dying!

Is this honest work? No, deep down inside the shipyard workers in India, the miners, the turkey farmers and even the care workers know that what they do is unethical. Fundamentally, you cannot pawn off responsibility on your employer. If you agree to work under unethical circumstances, of any kind, you become part of it. It takes two to tango.

Honest work consists in focusing on the task, being keen on providing quality and being truthful.

> Ethical case: A leader joined a program on alcohol rehabilitation and an employee was appointed for the position temporarily. When the leader returned to his job, he found it hard to pull himself together to attend the meetings for alcoholics anonymous. The employee sensed this and thus participated in the meetings with him, until he was ready to take over himself. This is an example of exceptional ethical performance.

Guidelines for the Ethical Employee:

- An Ethical employee is diligent and committed to his or her work
- An Ethical employee takes responsibility for the task given him or her
- An Ethical employee asks about the entity and understands the context
- An Ethical employee says no to work that can harm him or her, others or the environment
- An Ethical employee leads negative energy back to where it came from
- An Ethical employee always makes his or her influence count, even in small matters
- An Ethical employee knows that he or she is part of an entity – one Earth, one people – and acts accordingly in all that he or she does

Sebastian: What then are the most important skills for a leader to have?

Dalai Lama: The most important skills to have as a leader is to be truthful, honest and respectful. Leadership is about leading people, and the proper way to lead people is not by force, but by trust, respect and honesty. To be a great leader you should also have humility and humbleness.

Sebastian: Do you think that some people have a certain talent for leadership?

Dalai Lama: Amongst humanity there are so very many different mental dispositions. From my point of view we need a variety of traditions and a variety of religions, because of these different mental dispositions.

The ability to lead may vary from person to person. Whether it is genetic, due to karma or some other reason, like high intelligence for instance, is not so important.

Like the plan behind trees, humans, animals and all the laws of nature, there must be someone or something that does the planning (laughs).

Anyway, whether it is due to genes, God or karma, there are many different abilities and forms of intelligence. All human beings basically have the same potential, but there are some differences. In the Buddhist tradition it is said that there are some qualities that you acquire from birth and some you can learn later on in life.

Of course it makes a big difference how you are brought up. To me it seems logical that some people, by nature, have more abilities to lead. They are more com-

petent in understanding the complexity of the task. But, I must admit, it seems that sometimes leaders are more aggressive and also more savage than others.

Society in general has become increasingly more competitive. Humility has become a scarce commodity.

People think – and wrongly so – that to be humble is the same as being a doormat. A leader who lets himself be pushed around is seen as a weak and inefficient leader. Maybe the reason for this misinterpretation of humility is to be found in the fact that the majority of people in ancient societies were less educated and had less access to proper information. Therefore the leaders could be more aggressive and impose more savage rules. In modern society the general population is better informed and better educated, and I think that the aggressive leaders are not so accepted anymore.

For me, the most important aspect in a leader is his or her ability to think holistically and to use intelligence to be visionary. That is not only important in leadership, but for everything and everyone, everywhere. If everyone had a holistic view on life many things would be better. But for that to happen, we have to overcome many obstacles. For instance, think about the subsidies European farmers are getting. That makes them think only about themselves. They are not thinking about the global economy. So both in the case of business leadership and in politics, holistic perception through education is very important.

Sebastian: *Why is it that some people want to lead, while others seem more willing to be led?*

Dalai Lama: *The very concept of leadership comes about when there is someone to be led. An enlightened human being has no need to lead, but until we all reach that state we have to make sure that it is those best qualified who get to lead. Step one is to discover leadership qualities through examination and then, if it is a public position, have a democratic election.*

It would be good to make sure that the candidates have certain qualifications before the voting takes place. It is not an easy matter because if you only look at the qualifications, you can be misled. Some may have great qualifications on paper, but their behavior may be disturbing. I still believe that, whenever possible, it is best to choose leaders through election. When it is the people who elect the leaders and something goes wrong, then ultimately, the people themselves made that choice – and they have the power to change it again.

Sebastian: You recommend democracy in the election of as many leaders as possible.

Dalai Lama: Yes, that is the best way. But such a system is not flawless either. Sometimes a party recommends the name of a candidate without any of the qualifications we talked about. Then you only have him or her to elect. Truly speaking, from my point of view, some of the politicians both here in India and abroad, although they are very eloquent, lack inner quality. They don't have the true qualities for leadership. So it would be better to have a kind of a board who could examine their qualifications. Both the qualifications that we can measure through testing their knowledge and those which can only be felt but are so difficult to measure. Later on we need to observe the results of his or her leadership.

Sebastian: In business – if you have the money, you can buy a company – and then employees just have to deal with you. There is no election if you own the company.

How can your answer be applied to those circumstances?

Dalai Lama: I don't have a specific knowledge of leadership in business, but even there, it should be based on natural talent, combined with aspects such as honesty, truthfulness and humility. And a good deal of visionary intelligence.

Conclusion: The time for convenient treachery is over

> *'Man is a strange animal. He generally cannot read the handwriting on the wall until his back is up against it.'*
> (Adlai Stevenson)

Well, we are backed up against the wall.

We have no ethical gravity in the world today, which is why the news is full of chaos, suffering and catastrophes.

We need to use the feedback from the past and create sustainable solutions to the distribution of wealth – or there is no future. And although things look bleak for mankind, I know we can lift ourselves out of our greediness, fear and the shadows of convenient treachery.

Human ethics are woven into our genes as a collective behavioral code for all mankind to follow, and now we face the task of releasing this inner knowledge and living by it. The more people who choose to live by their own inner guidelines for proper ethical behavior, the more effect it will have on humankind and, like all processes of change, it is about reaching critical mass – when enough people do something, it determines our collective way of living.

THE WORLD IS A SMALL PLACE

The intercultural aspect of global life is becoming increasingly important with the sharing of information over the Internet, the easier and quicker ways to travel and the global outlook of contemporary business.

It is vital for modern businesses to accommodate cultural differences, in markets and with their employees. Differences create energy and can be positively channeled into the business through corporations if there is mutual respect between culturally diverse employees. It is very important for the global business leader to have an understanding of this.

To thrive on the energy created by cultural differences, businesses must make sure to treat all employees with equal respect, and thus create a solid foundation for positive creative co-operation between culturally differentiated employees. Otherwise the cultural differences will most likely have a negative impact on the organization.

Some progressive businesses have employees of up to 50 different nationalities and it is quite a task to integrate the various cultural traditions. But perhaps the knowledge and experience gained from these global forerunners can help the whole of humanity?

If we saw ourselves as The World Inc. – a global organization for all humanity – and set up a positively sustainable business vision for our common future, people could learn to work together – in a collective vision – with the globe as our common workplace and prosperous human lives for everyone as our product. Could we disarm prejudice by joining forces in finding our common heritage and future?

Information technology has already had a huge impact on our species. The world has become a smaller place as knowledge has become more widely accessible. It gives us hope that the process of globalization will strengthen a feeling of community across the world, regardless of culture, religion, age or gender.

> **Ethical case**: A number of Danish eye doctors regularly travel to third world countries at their own expense and operate on people with cataract. Cataract is the second biggest cause of blindness in the third world. The most common cause is a relatively simple infection that produces scar tissue in the eye. This, however, is very difficult to treat, once things have gone wrong. That is why eye doctors are working on a local initiative that inspires young eye surgeons to participate in these activities. This is also done without remuneration.
>
> Similarly, there is a group of veterinarians from Animal SOS who, at their own expense, travel to India to work around the clock taking care of street dogs. This work not only secures healthier dogs. Each year, many children die of rabies resulting from dog bites, and in the towns where the veterinarians have visited most often, that number has declined considerably.

But remember: less than ¼ of the world's population has access to the Internet (Source 1). The process has only just begun and needs every bit of help you can give it to continue along its course. No doubt numerous people will try to convince you that the whole thing is a utopia, but tell them this: 'The world is moving so fast today that someone telling you that something cannot be done – becomes doable while you say it!' (Source: Internet World Stats 2009 23.5% of the population has access to the Internet.)

Utopia

Only when we as a species start living our lives according to our ethical core principles, can the world change for the better.

When I give lectures on the world as it could be – were we to follow these inner guidelines for ethical behavior – I am typically met with four common responses from the audience:

The majority says, 'It is a beautiful dream, but a utopia'. With the world currently operating mostly on primitive human instincts of survival, strength and fear, it is understandable how it can be difficult to see it as a realistic near-future scenario. Nevertheless, I am absolutely convinced that raising the ethical awareness and consciousness of every human being, with all the responsibilities and possibilities that follow, is the only way forward to a brighter future for humanity.

How long it will take for the critical mass of humanity to realize this I cannot say, but I will dedicate myself to pushing the process along. When we finally manage to sway the majority we will no longer have a utopia, we will have real hope.

The second reaction is anger and contempt – aggressive angst, which has helped them suppress the frightening realization that so much of their life consists of coping strategies and lies.

The aggressive but controlled people in the audience even manage to cover up their anger with sarcastic tolerance and indirect aggressive comments, 'He doesn't have a clue about the real world, does he?'

The third and rarest response is that people actually reflect on the ideas and consider what changes they can implement in their own lives.

And then of course there is the fourth reaction: those who are very eager to be signed up immediately – to join the club, so to speak. Their enthusiasm is certainly very praiseworthy, but I sometimes curb their enthusiasm by explaining that it is not about wearing a pin stating that you are 'keeping it real' or getting your name engraved on a gold plaque. 'Keeping it real' means always living in harmony with the ethical notes emitted by our inner knowledge – there are no shortcuts and no memberships. Experience tells me that it is impossible to predict who is ready to take in the message and who isn't. The important thing is that people wake up and take responsibility when they are ready.

A top business leader recently sent me an email. It said: 'As you may remember I took part in one of your seminars on Emotional Intelligence eight years ago. I was the guy who during the workshop got up and exclaimed that your message of compassion and presence was sickening and had no place in modern business. I was really mad and demanded my money back – as a matter of principle. Your organization returned my fee without even blinking. Now I am writing to ask you to let me pay my fee for the seminar because it has finally dawned on me what you were talking about. Furthermore, I have incorporated your message from back then and used your code for authentic leadership in my organization and I am happy to report that it works – both for me and my employees.'

He took his time to come around, but what a wonderful human and humble response, which says a lot about that man.

If we lived in a perfect world scenario where everyone existed in harmony with the universal ethical values, we would, upon encountering something new, try to learn from it, and incorporate the new knowledge into our behavior. When you learn that something is wrong you take action to correct it. That is really all there is to it. But for most of us, there is often quite a delay between acknowledging something and acting according to that new knowledge.

Ethical case: A social worker who recently moved to the area gets a job at an institution for mentally challenged individuals – but already on her first day at work, she experiences how the staff is not acting respectfully around the residents. At lunch, one of the nurses imitates Mr. Smith, who is paranoid. Mr. Smith examines his shoes before putting them on, and the rest of the staff is loudly amused. The new employee says that she finds it inappropriate to laugh at the residents – to which the nurse replies, 'As long as it's done with a loving sense of humor, it doesn't matter, does it?' The rest of the employees start taking part in the discussion as well, and support the nurse's standpoint. The new employee, however, maintains that it is unethical and that it cannot be loving when you laugh at people, who are mentally disabled. One of the other employees says that, once she has also worked at the institution for 5-6 years, she too will get off her high horse. The new employee decides to have a talk with the leader about her experience. When she arrives for the meeting at the end of the day, the others have beaten her to it and said that they cannot work with her, because she seeks conflict and acts degradingly. In the end, the new social worker has to find a different job, as the others froze her out.

THERE IS HOPE

Our collective intelligence gives us the ability to control all the different environments that we encounter around the world.

Though we are not physically very fast compared to other animals we can use technology to travel further and faster than any other creature on Earth. We are not aquatic animals, yet we sail on the oceans and dive to the bottom of the sea. Despite our lack of wings we fly around the world and even into space.

Our ability to overcome obstacles, solve problems and liberate ourselves from past thinking is unique – if only we let ourselves think freely. Thanks to our species' technological development, we have transcended our natural biological fears. Otherwise we couldn't have conquered the seas, or the skies for that matter.

The mental development we have gone through is particularly impressive and nothing suggests that it should stop now. Unless of course we trip along the way, destroying the Earth and forever killing off the remaining hope of turning things around.

We are indeed our own worst enemy. And why is that? Because our ethical awareness has not kept pace with our mental development. But there is hope when the economist Muhammed Yunus can receive Nobel's peace price in 2006 for his idea of micro loans – which, since then, has spread across the entire globe.

We are people of the Earth. We own businesses, run businesses, do our jobs and exist in the global society. I hope that Pure Business, True Leadership and Honest Work will grow to become natural standards that everyone will follow in the future.

The differences in our life conditions and resources might be obvious, but setting that aside, if we follow the Fundamental Human Code, the world will surely become a better place.

And it all starts with you. In the end every human being must decide for him or herself whether or not to live ethically in concordance with the universal values. The responsibility lies with you.

> **Ethical case**: A new president takes office after the previous one has undermined practically all ethical core values, but rather than directing his anger towards that individual – he simply starts cleaning up and says no to torture, anarchy and illegal prisoners, etc. There is hope.

IT IS A MYSTERY TO LIVE

'Life is not a problem to solve – it's a mystery to live', said Italian psychologist Roberto Assagioli, bringing up one of the big questions – or perhaps even one of the big traumas – of human existence.

To me it seems like most people are engaged with solving problems instead of experiencing the adventure of life. Of course when you are living in poverty and struggling to survive, you may not find life particularly magical. But those of us who do not have to worry about the next meal or shelter for our family still focus entirely on solving problems, on making a profit and hoarding it while life itself passes us by unnoticed.

We are so busy consuming that we forget to exist. And yet, at the same time, we see more and more people moving towards global awareness – gaining a holistic perspective on existence.

Every culture has wrestled the big existentialist questions: who am I and why am I here? In the short time we have occupied this planet we have seen one civilization after another reign supreme only to fall from grace and disappear. Most, because they ignored the warning signals: the Aztecs, the Incas, the Egyptians and the Greek empire are just a few of those civilizations that have perished as such.

We possess the wisdom that the collective human race has accumulated, but we do not utilize it fully. When we do, it will secure a strong foundation for everything to come.

Modern information technology makes it possible to exchange knowledge globally. In time, everyone on Earth will be able to access our combined consciousness through the Internet: Earth's communal database.

The dream would be that all history and all human knowledge and wisdom is indexed in an enormous uncensored library fully accessible to everyone. That way nobody would be kept in the dark as to the rights and possibilities of every human being.

Unfortunately, with companies such as Google and Yahoo bowing to China's demands, that those inside China cannot search certain words such as 'human rights', this is still a dream, which is yet to be fully realized.

A New Dawn

'The future is inevitable – progress is not.' Those wise words once came from Danish philosopher, Poul Henningsen. The future will come to us no matter what. The real challenge is to find the courage and collectively make the right choices to ensure that our common future becomes our common progress.

I am thoroughly convinced that every human has the capacity for self-exploration and so the door is open to the new time – a new time when each person will take responsibility for their own lives – in mind, body and spirit – both locally, as a group and globally. It is about time we all stopped trying to put the blame on somebody else, and instead took responsibility for changing what we can!

When we each understand how we are all part of a collective field of energy, our egocentric practices of times past will give way to human fellowship. Like a global epiphany, it will change everything and give us the much-needed hope for the future.
With the dark shadows over human history one could question our eligibility as a species. Hate, cruelty, humiliation and fear have become the henchmen who walk silently beside us.

But, as mentioned in the opening of the book, in my experience most people sense that something is wrong in the world today.

What we need here on Earth is not renewal or change – we need a total transformation.

Nothing less than to release our full inner potential, rise above our primitive past, always follow our ethical DNA, take responsibility for each other and for all life.

Only then can we take the step up the evolutionary ladder and develop a sustainable future on our one globe – as one people. And as long as one person hopes, there is hope for all of us.

As long as one person can reach out and forgive his fellow man, the soul of humanity is intact.

As long as one person knows that his or her soul lives forever, wisdom lives in eternity – and so does humanity.

It is not just about courage or sacrifice, for we simply have no choice if mankind shall continue to exist. If we stubbornly adhere to the old ways and paradigms, we will atrophy in our current identity of egotism, fear and unrealized potential.

The key is for every human being to listen to his or her inner ethical voice and let that voice serve as our common foundation for a new global society.

> **Ethical case**: I am standing at the till about to pay. A married couple is ahead of me and it is obvious that they are not doing well. The woman in particular looks sad and withdrawn. I pick one of the flowers I have just purchased – look her in the eyes and say, 'Here you go' … She accepts the flower and it is as if her face cracks and a smile appears.
>
> That's all it takes … Do what you can each day …

Sebastian: Why is it that even though the motive of a leader is pure and from the heart, sometimes people perceive his or her actions as negative? In leadership you have to make decisions and other people may disagree or become angry, while you know that you strive to do the right thing. What can you do?

Dalai Lama: The perspective in leadership is sometimes long-termed, and that might mean that you sometimes make some short-term sacrifices. If you as a leader have a long-term interest and, as we discussed before, a more holistic consciousness, some people may not see that. But you have to look at it from case to case.

Take, for example the Tibetan problem. Our way of approach is not to seek total independence, but to go for general autonomy. I know that many Tibetans feel that that is a mistake. Some of the youth organizations disagree with our approach. They want us to seek total independence, and they say that our approach is a terrible mistake.

But that is the natural dilemma of leadership.

I believe that the most important thing in good leadership is to be truthful, honest and to have a long-term vision for your actions. You must try to explain the reasons for your actions, and show that your motivation is very sincere. If you do that then I think that the majority of any group of people, who are sensible, will understand and therefore come to appreciate your actions.

But there will often be some part of a group who will not, or cannot, agree to your decisions. In our case, some of the Tibetan youths are very emotional about wanting independence and they continue to say that our approach is a mistake even though we have explained to them that we have good reasons for this. We will of course continue to explain our long-term view to them and even though they may not easily accept our point of view emotionally, they may come to understand it intellectually. We will never stop trying to make them understand the reasons for our approach in this matter.

Sebastian: So your approach to those who disagree is to make them understand from a logical point of view. Emotionally they may still find it difficult to accept, but at least they understand the reasons.

Dalai Lama: Yes. Let me give you another example. We have had meetings with Chinese officials, both on an official and a more private level. On all occasions when we have met face-to-face, we have spoken the truth, disregarding the level of the meeting. We have stayed true to what we believe is right, no matter how aggressive the dialog has been and that has proven to be the best position. They have often remained defensive, because we have spoken the truth. But we have to tread carefully because if something goes wrong in these meetings, then the lives of the people living inside Tibet could become even more difficult, because the Chinese often deal with things in a hard manner.

If you stand on an unethical foundation, you will always have difficulties. You might be able to deceive yourself for a while, but in the long run you cannot succeed. Alternatively, if you state your reasons with self-confidence – and your interests are in a larger holistic perspective – i.e. not held out of self-centeredness or own personal interest – you will always have a strong foundation. If you, at the same time, work sincerely for the people around you, you can face any challenge.

Life is yours – for ever and ever

To counteract what you may have heard before, I have composed a new Creed based on what IS ... i.e. the eternal solidarity ... with everything ... because this insight will dissolve the shadows that may have descended upon the wisdom of your soul ... and free you to independently choose ... your life ...

I am

"I am who I am...I have always been who I am...and I will always be who I am.

In this inferno of fear and greed ... in this incarnation that started out in darkness ... I had forgotten who I am ... a heavy load of lies came to overshadow the memory of who I am ... and that is when I thought that I was this one *person ... who had this one life to live ...and the fear descended upon my soul's eternal wisdom ... and everything turned dark ... my days were filled with meaningless actions with no direction ... whose sole purpose was to contain me, so that others ... who were also scared, could gain a sense of security ...*

Faith in life was replaced by fear of not being able to meet my own needs ... I forgot that we are all woven together in flesh, blood and spirit ... that we share the same forefathers here on Earth ... that we belong to one shining people ... that man is not the drop ... but part of the vast ocean ... that all energy is one unbreakable entity ...

For a while, my clear, inner voice was drowned by the noise of fear ... my inner self where eternity reigns ... where the energy gives me direction ... where God speaks to me ... and everything comes together as one ...

The greed took over and vanity briefly soothed my immense need ... I stuffed myself with materialistic things and sedated my soul's innate sense of direction ... my congenital, ethical compass was ... for a brief moment out of order ... and the illusion of loneliness drew me towards other overshadowed, lonely souls, and we called it love ... even when the lie resonated hollowly, we promised each other to be eternally faithful ...

For a brief moment filled with fear, I had forgotten everything ... THAT IS ... and I saw how some people surrounded themselves with power as a protection against despair, and how others looked on ... while their relatives charred in the powerlessness of poverty ... without doing anything ...

I forgot about the wisdom of the heart ... and let myself be put off with empty words and false proof ... I had forgotten that I was created of eternal energy and that no one can come between it and me ... I had forgotten that no one else knows my way to eternity ... to God ... and that those who say they do, serve no one but themselves ...

I had forgotten that, deep within each person is a key ... a special code that only God knows ... by which he recognizes me ... I had forgotten that each person is in direct contact with the energy of eternity ... with God ... and with all life ... and everything living ... I had forgotten who I am ... in a brief moment of fear, I had forgotten who I am ...

... But in this shining moment, NOW, I recognize who I AM ..."

If we base our lives on an unethical foundation, we will always experience great difficulties – even if we manage to fool ourselves for a while. But, in the long run, it is not possible to build a sustainable future on an uneven foundation.

Alternatively, we can choose to live a life that is based on our innate ethical fundamental nature, and when our decisions are based on a higher holistic perspective on solidarity – meaning that these are not based on egoism or selfishness – our foundation will always be stronger. Once we are able to live with – not of – our environment, we will be able to realize the potential of the embedded genius that lies within us all and then we can overcome ant challenge. The choice is yours – now.

References

Almaas, A. H. 'Essence with The Elixir of Enlightenment: The Diamond Approach to Inner Realization'. Red Wheel / Weiser, 1998

Almaas, A. H. 'Diamond Heart, Book Four: Indestructible Innocence'. Shambhala, 2000.

Almaas, A. H. 'Diamond Heart, Book Three: Being and the Meaning of Life'. Shambhala, 2000.

Almaas, A. H. 'Diamond Heart, Book Two: The Freedom to Be'. Shambhala, 2000.

Almaas, A. H. 'Diamond Heart, Book One: Elements of the Real in Man'. Shambhala, 2000.

Andersen, Kirstine. Kierkegaard og ledelse

Arthur, James Ray. Practical Spirituality: How to Use Spiritual Power to Create Tangible Results, 2005

Assagioli, Roberto. Psychosynthesis, 1971 The Act of Will: A Guide to Self-Actualization & Self-Realization, 1999

Assayas, Michka. 'Bono: In Conversation with Michka Assayas'. Riverhead Hardcover, 2005.

Bauer, Joachim. Warum ich fühle, was du fühlst. Hoffmann und Campe Verlag, Hamburg, 2005.

Boniwell, Ilona. Positive Spychology in a Nutshell.

Carr, Alan: Positive Psychology.

Charnys, Geoffroi de: (Niels Tenberg, ed.). Le livre de Chevalerie, 1352. Roskilde University Press, 1996.

Christopher, Frith & Wolpert, Daniel. The Neuroscience of Social Interaction: Decoding, Imitating, and Influencing the Actions of Others. Edited New York: Oxford University Press, 2004.

Coffman, Curt & Gonzalez-Molina, Gabriel. Follow this Path: How the World's Greatest Organizations Drive Growth by Unleashing Human Potential.

Cooperrider, Sorensen, Yeager, Whitney. Appreciative Inquiry.

Dalai Lama. 'The World of Tibetan Buddhism: An Overview of Its Philosophy and Practice'. Wisdom Publications, 1995.

Dalai Lama and Nicholas Vreeland (Editor) 'An Open Heart: Practicing Compassion in Everyday Life'. Little, Brown and Company, 2001.

Dalai Lama. 'Ethics for the New Millennium'. Riverhead Trade, 2001.

Dalai Lama. 'The Universe in a Single Atom: The Convergence of Science and Spirituality'. Broadway, 2006.

Dalai Lama and Howard C. Cutler. 'The Art of Happiness: A Handbook for Living'. Riverhead Hardcover, 1998.

Dalai Lama. 'How to See Yourself As You Really Are'. Atria, Reprint edition, 2007.

Dalai Lama. 'Consciousness at the Crossroads: Conversations with the Dalai Lama on Brainscience and Buddhism'. Snow Lion Publications, 1999.

Dalai Lama. Meditation til det nye årtusinde.

Dalai Lama. Tanker for det nye årtusinde.

Diamond, Jared. Collapse: How Societies Choose to Fail or Succeed, 2005

Diamond, Jared. The Third Chimpanzee. The Evolution and Future of the Human Animal. New York. HarperCollins, 1991

Einhorn, Stefan. Kunsten at være et godt menneske, 2006

Frank, Lone. Den femte revolution, 2007

Gandhi, Mahatma and Mahadev H. Desai. 'Gandhi – An Autobiography: The Story of My Experiments With Truth'. Beacon Press, 1993.

Gardner, Howard. De mange intelligensers pædagogik, 1998

Gladwell, Malcolm. Det magiske vendepunkt, 2002

Gladwell, Malcolm. Blink, 2006

Goldberg, Elkhonon. Visdommens Paradoks, 2005

Goleman, Daniel. Destructive Emotions: A Scientific Dialogue with the Dalai Lama, 2003. Healing Emotions: Conversations with the Dalai Lama on Mindfulness, Emotions, and Health, 1997.

Groves, Dawn. Lær at forstå og praktisere meditation, 2000

Gyatso, Ven Lobsang. 'The Four Noble Truths'. Snow Lion Publications, 1994.

Hanh, Thich Nhat. 'The Diamond That Cuts Through Illusion: Commentaries on the Prajnaparamita Diamond Sutra'. Parallax Press, 1992.

Hanh, Thich Nhat. 'The Heart of the Buddha's Teaching'. Broadway; New Ed edition, 1999

HH the Dalai Lama & Jeffrey Hopkins. How to Practice – the Way to a Meaningful Life, Simon & Schuster, 2002.

Illeris, Knud. Læring, 1999

Jensen, Peter K. A. Menneskets oprindelse og udvikling. Gads forlag, 1996.

Jung. Tekster & tanker.

Knoop, Hans Henrik & Jørgen Lyhne. Et nyt læringslandskab.

Kringelbach, Morten L. Hjernerum – Den følelsesfulde hjerne.

Ridderstråle, Jonas & Nordström, Kjell A. Karaoke Kapitalisme, 2003.

Lave, Jean & Wenger, Etienne. Situated Learning, Legimate Peripheral Participation, Cambridge

University Press, 1991.

Leman, Kevin. Dit nummer i søskenderækken, 2004

Mandela, Nelson. 'Long Walk to Freedom: The Autobiography of Nelson Mandela'. Back Bay Books; 1st Paperback edition, 1995.

Mandrup, Charlotte. Mindfulness / Mindfulness i hverdagen / Erik & Autoritet i lederskabet.

Morris, Desmond. The Human Zoo / The Naked Abe.

Nybo, Sebastian. Det Indre Lederskab.

Nybo, Sebastian. Ro, Balance og Indsigt.

Pease, Allan & Barbara. Kropssprog.

Rinbochay, Lati. 'Mind in Tibetan Buddhism'. Snow Lion Publications, 1981.

Seligman, Martin E. P. Authentic Happiness, 2004. Authentic Happiness Using the New Positive Psychology to Realize Your Potential for Lasting, 2003

Seligman, Martin E. P., Joseph, Stephen & Linley, P. Alex: Positive Psychology in Practice, 2004

Sheldon, K. M., Elliot, A. J., Kim, Y., & Kasser, T. What Is Satisfying about Satisfying Events? Testing 10 Candidate Psychological Needs. Journal of Personality and Social Psychology, 80(2), 325-339, 2001.

Simple-living.dk. Nye veje til et enkelt liv.

Snyder, Lopez. Handbook of Positive Psychology, 2004

Sovik, Rolf. Moving Inward – the journey to meditation.

St. James, Elaine. Simplify Your Life.

Stamenov, Maksim and Gallese, Vittorio. Mirror Neurons and the Evolution of Brain and Language

Edited Amsterdam, Neth., John Benjamins Publishing, 2002

Tolle, Eckhart. 'A New Earth: Awakening to Your Life's Purpose'. Penguin, 2008.

Tolle, Eckhart. 'A New Earth'. Penguin Books Ltd, 2006.

Tolle, Eckhart. 'Practicing the Power of Now: Essential Teachings, Meditations, and Exercises from The Power of Now'. New World Library, 2001.

Tolle, Eckhart. 'The Power of Now: A Guide to Spiritual Enlightenment'. New World Library, 2004.

Vedfelt, Ole. Ubevidst intelligens, du ved mere end du tror.

Wilson, David Sloan. 'Evolution for Everyone: How Darwin's Theory Can Change the Way We Think About Our Lives'. Delta; Reprint edition, 2007.

Wolf, Fred Alan. Dr. Quantum's Little Book Of Big Ideas: Where Science Meets Spirit. Mind into Matter: A New Alchemy of Science.

Authour biographies

ABOUT SEBASTIAN NYBO

Sebastian Nybo is a Professional Psychological Consultant, Master of Talent, and the Founder and Managing Director of SEB Gruppen A/S in Copenhagen, Denmark. In addition to writing this book, "Be generous and prosper", he is also the author of "Inner Leadership" and "How to Deal with Difficult People".

Sebastian's break with conventional thinking is always insightful and provocative. Over the past 18 years he has taught more than 95,000 people in Denmark and abroad, and his consultancy has ensured high performance in turnaround processes for a number of businesses, such as LEGO, Novo, Deloitte, Ellos, Google, and many more.

His hands-on knowledge, based on his experience, is integrated with a continued in-depth study of human psychology, which offers him a practical and holistic angle for his presentation. Through collaborative partnerships with an international network of researchers and theorists in psychology, philosophy, and communication, he has built a strong and unconventional foundation. For more information, please visit www.wisdominaction.nu.

Through his work, Sebastian Nybo has specialized in the following topics: Self-Management (described in the book "Inner Leadership"), Conflict Management 2.0 (described in the book "How to Handle Difficult People") and CSR or Professional Ethics described in the book. Sebastian Nybo has shown particular strength as a ground-breaking visionary in empowering people to take charge of their own lives and circumstances.

His professional range derives from his willingness to launch new projects and he manages to weave together professional consultancy and a scientific approach to spirituality to build a solid foundation for decision-making. Sebastian Nybo is known for his intense presence, his direct manner, and his ability to simplify complex concepts using humor and imagery.

About His Holiness the 14th Dalai Lama

His Holiness the Dalai Lama, Tenzin Gyatso, is the Tibetans' religious leader. Born in 1935, he was recognized as the rebirth of the 13th Dalai Lama when he was two years old. His Holiness began his monastic education at the age of six. The curriculum consisted of five major and five minor subjects. The major subjects were logic, Tibetan art and culture, Sanskrit, medicine, and Buddhist philosophy, which was divided into five categories: Prajnaparimita, the perfection of wisdom; Madhyamika, the philosophy of the middle way; Vinaya, the canon of monastic discipline; Abidharma, metaphysics; and Pramana, logic and epistemology. The five minor subjects were poetry, music and drama, astrology, motre and phrasing, and synonyms. At the age of 23 he sat for his final examination in the Jokhang Temple, Lhasa, during the annual Monlam (prayer) Festival in 1959. He passed with honors and was awarded the Geshe Lharampa degree, the highest-level degree equivalent to a doctorate of Buddhist philosophy.

Since China's invasion in 1949, H.H. the Dalai Lama has lived in exile in northern India and has worked tirelessly for peace and non-violent coexistence. In 1954, he went to Beijing for peace talks with Mao Zedong and other Chinese leaders, including Deng Xiaoping and Chou Enlai. But finally, in 1959, following the brutal suppression of the Tibetan national uprising in Lhasa by Chinese troops, His Holiness was forced to escape into exile. Since then he has lived in Dharamsala, northern India, the seat of the Tibetan political administration.

In 1963 he founded the Democratic constitution "The Charter of the Tibetans-in-Exile". Since 1959 he has received numerous prizes, honorary doctorates, and other acknowledgments for his message about freedom, inter-religious understanding, universal understanding, and compassion. Since the Chinese invasion, His Holiness has appealed to the United Nations on the question of Tibet. The General Assembly adopted three resolutions on Tibet in 1959, 1961, and 1965. Throughout his life, he has encouraged peace and non-violence, for which he received the Nobel Peace Prize in 1989.

His Holiness the Dalai Lama is the author or co-author of more than 75 books. For more information, please visit www.dalailam.com" www.dalailam.com

अनन्याः सन्ति ॥
There are no others
(Ramana Maharshi)